THE
WONDER
OF HEAVEN

RON RHODES

HARVEST HOUSE PUBLISHERS

EUGENE, OREGON

Cover by Dugan Design Group, Bloomington, Minnesota

THE WONDER OF HEAVEN
Copyright © 2009 by Ron Rhodes
Published by Harvest House Publishers
Eugene, Oregon 97402
www.harvesthousepublishers.com

Library of Congress Cataloging-in-Publication Data
    Rhodes, Ron.
    The wonder of heaven / Ron Rhodes.
        p. cm.
    Includes bibliographical references.
    ISBN 978-0-7369-2456-6 (pbk.)
    1. Heaven—Christianity. I. Title.
    BT846.3.R46 2009
    236.'24—dc22
                                                                            2008020677

Printed in the United States of America

09 10 11 12 13 14 15 16 17 / BP-NI / 10 9 8 7 6 5 4 3 2 1

With fond memories of my brother Paul...
now absent from the body, at home with the Lord.

2 CORINTHIANS 5:8

Acknowledgments

Special heartfelt thanks go to my wife, Kerri, and our two children, David and Kylie. How I look forward to living with them for all eternity in the unimaginably splendorous "heavenly country" (Hebrews 11:16)! Thanks also to my many friends at Harvest House Publishers, especially Bob Hawkins Jr., for his continued commitment to publishing relevant, contemporary books.

Anticipating Heaven

"Whatever pleasures we have known here on earth while living under the curse of sin are trivial, paltry diversions compared to the pure delights of heaven."

—John MacArthur

"We will be ageless and not know pain, tears, sorrow, sickness, or death. We will have bodies of splendor."

—Rene Pache

"We shall then have joy without sorrow, and rest without weariness.... Be of good cheer, Christian, the time is near, when God and thou shalt be near, and as near as thou canst well desire. Thou shalt dwell in his family."

—Richard Baxter

"The king of terrors, the last enemy, will never be able to breach the pearly gates and disturb the bliss of heaven! No more deathbed vigils or funerals. The hearse will have made its last journey."

—J. Oswald Sanders

"Let us not be afraid to meditate often on the subject of heaven, and to rejoice in the prospect of good things to come.... Let us take comfort in the remembrance of the other side."

—J.C. Ryle

"For Christians, death on its earthward side is simply that the tired mortal body falls temporarily to sleep, while on the heavenward side we suddenly find ourselves with our dear Savior-King and with other Christian loved ones in the heavenly home. Why fear that?"

—J. Sidlow Baxter

"When we get to Heaven, the joy of seeing our loved ones once again is immeasurably increased when we realize that all of us will indeed be perfect! There will be no more disagreements or cross words, hurt feelings or misunderstandings, neglect or busyness, interruptions or rivalry, jealousy or pride, selfishness or sin of any kind!"

—ANNE GRAHAM LOTZ

"Heavenly-mindedness is sanity. It is the best regimen for keeping our hearts whole, our minds clear.... It allows us to endure life's agonies without despair."

—MARK BUCHANAN

"Resolved, to endeavor to my utmost to act as I can think I should do, if I had already seen the happiness of heaven…"

—JONATHAN EDWARDS

"There is a land of pure delight,
    Where saints immortal reign;
Infinite day excludes the night,
    And pleasures banish pain."

—"THERE IS A LAND OF PURE DELIGHT" (HYMN)

"I want to know one thing:
    the way to heaven—how to land
    safe on that happy shore.
God Himself has condescended to teach the way;
    for this very end He came from heaven.
He has written it down in a book.
    Oh, give me that book!
    At any price give me that book!
I have it—here is knowledge enough for me.
    Let me be a man of one book.
Here, then, I am, far from the busy ways of men.
    I sit down alone; only God is here.
In His presence I open and read His book
    that I may find the way to heaven."

—JOHN WESLEY

CONTENTS

THE WONDER OF HEAVEN

In the Shakespearean play *Hamlet*, death—and what lies beyond death's door—is metaphorically described as "the undiscovered country."[1] It seems an appropriate way of describing something that human beings know so very little about.

The Scriptures use the word "country" of the blissful, eternal ream of heaven. Indeed, the splendorous abode where saints will one day dwell is described as a heavenly country (Hebrews 11:16)—and the saints will dwell there for *all eternity*.

Eternity is a big concept. We read in the pages of Holy Writ that God has "set eternity in the hearts of men" (Ecclesiastes 3:11). This inspiring verse led one commentator to reflect, "Though living in a world of time, man has intimations of eternity. Instinctively he thinks of 'forever,' and though he cannot understand the concept, he realizes that beyond this life there is the possibility of a shoreless ocean of time."[2] It is wondrous to even think about it. It is in view of this sense of eternity in the human heart that one

Christian suggested that "we're heaven-bent," that "our hearts have an inner tilt upward," and that "the grain of our souls leans heavenward."[3] I think he is right!

From the first book in the Bible to the last, we read of great men and women of God who gave evidence that eternity permeated their hearts. We read of people like Abel, Enoch, Noah, Abraham, and David—each yearning to live with God in eternity. David, in particular, put it this way: "As the deer pants for streams of water, so my soul pants for you, O God. My soul thirsts for God, for the living God. *When can I go and meet with God?*" (Psalm 42:1-2, emphasis added). He rejoiced, saying, "I will dwell in the house of the LORD forever" (Psalm 23:6).

Speaking of the blessed saints Abel, Enoch, Noah, and Abraham, Scripture reveals the following:

> They admitted that they were aliens and strangers on earth. People who say such things show that they are looking for a country of their own. If they had been thinking of the country they had left, they would have had opportunity to return. Instead, they were longing for a *better* country—a *heavenly* one. Therefore God is not ashamed to be called their God, for *he has prepared a city for them* (Hebrews 11:13-16, emphasis added).

These saints realized that this world was not their final home. "They were content to be strangers and pilgrims, refusing the urge to nestle to make themselves comfortable. Their desire was to pass through the world without taking any of its character upon themselves. Their hearts were set on pilgrimage."[4] Refusing to be distracted, these saints "saw the promised realities from a distance and persisted in their pilgrim character, looking for a country of their own and refusing to return to the land they had left."[5]

In much the same way, Christians throughout church history have longed for heaven's joys, considering themselves to be only loosely tied to this earth.[6] No wonder the great J.C. Ryle (A.D. 1816–1900) suggested that "believers are in a strange land...in the life to come they will be at home."[7] At the moment of death, you and I as Christians literally depart the land of the dying to go to the land of the truly living.

The Near Universal Belief in an Afterlife

All throughout human history, people of different cultures and religions have given evidence that they possessed a sense of eternity in their hearts. As Randy Alcorn puts it in his book *Heaven*, "Anthropological evidence suggests that every culture has a God-given, innate sense of the eternal—that this world is not all there is."[8] Because of this innate sense of eternity, Barry Morrow suggests that "from earliest times humanity has tenaciously believed in an afterlife."[9] We see this even in false religions.[10] Islam, for example, speaks of a sensual paradise, while Native American religions speak of eternal hunting grounds. In Confucianism, when a parent dies, the children must perform all necessary rituals so that the parent can enjoy a trouble-free afterlife. Children thus burn a paper house, car, money, and other such items in order to transfer them to their deceased loved one in the afterlife. Modern psychics have built an entire religion on belief in an afterlife. Though such false religions have grossly distorted the truth about the afterlife, it is nevertheless highly revealing that belief in some form of an afterlife is near-universal.

This near-universal belief is surely the reason, as Thomas Ice and Timothy Demy point out, that "throughout the centuries, heaven has been depicted by artists and poets, authors and preachers. Augustine, Dante, John Milton, John Bunyan, C.S. Lewis, and scores of others have written on heaven and its glories." Indeed,

Ice and Demy note, heaven is "sung about in hymns, spirituals, classical music, and country and western music. It is spoken of in jokes and in sermons, in hospitals and in classrooms."[11]

This great interest in the mystery of the afterlife continues today. Christian pastor Mark Hitchcock notes that the Discovery Channel featured a program about the ten great mysteries of the world. "The mysteries included the lost city of Atlantis, UFOs, Bigfoot, Stonehenge, and the Loch Ness Monster. But the over-whelming number one mystery was life after death."[12]

How is it with you, my Christian friend? Are you interested in heaven and the afterlife? Do you long for a "better country," a *heavenly* country? Do you ever spend time pondering what heaven might be like? If so, you're my kind of person, and this book is for you!

Contemplating What Heaven Might Be Like

Each of us likely already has an idea regarding what heaven might be like. The chances are, though, that our culturally influenced conceptions are woefully inadequate to capture the full glory and splendor of what truly awaits the children of God in the afterlife. One Christian who lived in the 1800s put it this way:

> In meditating upon the happiness in store for the children of God, we are very apt to build up a heaven of our own, which naturally takes the shape and color which our sorrows, needs, and sufferings lend thereto. The poor man, for instance, who has suffered much from toil and want, looks upon heaven as a place of rest, abounding with all that can satisfy the cravings of nature. Another, who has often endured the pangs of disease, looks upon it as a place where he shall enjoy perpetual health of body and mind. Again another,

who in the practice of virtue, has had all manner of temptations from the devil, the world, and his own flesh, delights in viewing heaven as a place totally free from temptation, where the danger, or even the possibility, of sin, shall be no more.

All these, and other similar views of heaven, are true, inasmuch as they represent it as a place entirely free from evil and suffering, and, at the same time, as an abode of positive happiness. Nevertheless, they are all imperfect views because not one of them takes in the whole of heavenly bliss, such as God has revealed it to us.[13]

God's revelation about heaven is found in the pages of holy Scripture. And what we find in Scripture is *firsthand, eyewitness* testimony about the divine abode. Jesus Himself came from heaven, and He testified of its existence, saying that it is the place His Father resides (John 1:14; 6:33-42,51,58; 8:42; 16:27-30). The apostle Paul was caught up to heaven to receive special revelation from God (2 Corinthians 12:1-4). Though some of what he saw and heard was apparently so overwhelming and ineffable that he was not permitted by God to reveal it to humans, what he *does* reveal is wondrous indeed (see, for example, Ephesians 1:10; Philippians 2:10; 3:20; Colossians 1:5,16,20; 3:1-2; 1 Thessalonians 1:10; 4:16; 2 Thessalonians 1:7). Finally, the apostle John received a vision of heaven that is recorded in substantial detail in the book of Revelation (see, especially, chapters 21 and 22).[14] From such eyewitnesses we not only gain assurance *that* heaven exists, but we are also privileged to learn many fascinating details about what it is like. I will address these details throughout this book. First, however, we must confront the preliminary truth of human mortality.

The Brevity of Earthly Life

The Bible consistently emphasizes the brevity of earthly life. The years pass so quickly. As I write, I am consciously aware of the sobering reality that more of my life is behind me than ahead of me. We are all aware of our mortality. Dr. Billy Graham, now in his nineties, was asked by an interviewer what surprised him most about life. Without hesitation, he replied, "Its brevity."[15] Life is short. And it seems that the older we get, the faster the time passes.

Addressing the brevity of life, Dr. Martyn Lloyd-Jones comments that "the moment you come into this world you are beginning to go out of it."[16] His point, of course, is that the moment we are born, the inevitable and relentless process toward death begins. None of us is exempt.

It is no wonder that Job, the great Old Testament servant of God, said that "man born of woman is of few days" (Job 14:1). He appealed to God, "Remember, O God, that my life is but a breath" (7:7). Just as a breath of vapor dissipates quickly on a cold day, so our lives seem all too short.

The psalmist thus pondered before God, "You have made my days a mere handbreadth; the span of my years is as nothing before you. Each man's life is but a breath" (Psalm 39:5). Reflecting back over his life, he said, "My days vanish like smoke" (102:3).

The New Testament continues this emphasis on man's brevity. In James 4:14 we are told, "You do not even know what will happen tomorrow. What is your life? You are a mist that appears for a little while and then vanishes." First Peter 1:24 likewise instructs us that "all men are like grass, and all their glory is like the flowers of the field; the grass withers and the flowers fall."

This is the struggle we must all face and deal with. Life is short. The days relentlessly pass. We grow old so quickly. And then we die.

It is a sobering exercise to ponder that, should the Lord delay His coming, not only I but my beloved wife and two precious children will one day be lowered into the earth in burial. If that were the end of things, then how despondent life would be. But, praise God, we will be reunited and live forever in the heavenly country, the eternal city of our beloved God (Hebrews 11:16). What a precious and glorious hope this is!

We Don't Know *When* We Will Die

Aside from the terminally ill who are at the final stage of their illness, none of us knows when we will die. The Old Testament patriarch Isaac once said, "I am now an old man and don't know the day of my death" (Genesis 27:2).

Some, however, die at a younger age. We read in Ecclesiastes 9:12 that "no man knows when his hour will come: As fish are caught in a cruel net, or birds are taken in a snare, so men are trapped by evil times that fall unexpectedly upon them." In Proverbs 27:1 the wise man therefore urged, "Do not boast about tomorrow, for you do not know what a day may bring forth." Each new day may bring the prospect of death.

For this reason, the wise person maintains a consistent awareness of his mortality so that he makes good use of the time God has graciously given. The psalmist accordingly prayed, "Show me, O LORD, my life's end and the number of my days; let me know how fleeting is my life" (Psalm 39:4). Those who maintain such an awareness live with deliberation and with appreciation for each new day. Time is a precious gift!

Our Lives Are in God's Hands

We naturally want to live as long as possible. But the actual timing of our deaths is in the hands of our sovereign God. He has allotted a certain time on earth for each of us. As Job said to God, "Man's days are determined; you have decreed the number of his months and have set limits he cannot exceed" (Job 14:5).

The apostle Paul in like manner said that God "himself gives all men life and breath and everything else. From one man he made every nation of men, that they should inhabit the whole earth; and *he determined the times set for them* and the exact places where they should live" (Acts 17:25-26, emphasis added). Perhaps Paul was thinking of the words of the psalmist: "All the days ordained for me were written in your book before one of them came to be" (Psalm 139:16).

As Christians, we need not worry about the day death will occur. Our God, who loves us infinitely, is in charge of the timing of our rendezvous with death, and we can trust Him completely. With the psalmist, we can restfully affirm, "My times are in your hands" (Psalm 31:15). We can count on the fact that we are *immortal* up until the time we have accomplished all that God intends for us to accomplish. Once that work is complete, God calls us home!

I recognize that this goes against our common understanding of "untimely" deaths. When a person dies in a car wreck, for example, we say that this person's death was untimely, and refer to the event as a tragic "accident." However, there are no accidents in God's sovereign timing (Isaiah 46:10; Acts 2:23; Ephesians 1:11). We can take comfort in this truth, because when a Christian loved one dies in such an "accident," we can rest assured that he or she died according to God's precise sovereign timing.[17] We still mourn (1 Thessalonians 4:13), but our grief is tempered by our awareness of God's sovereign oversight of all earthly affairs. He is in charge (Psalm 21:1; 22:28; 139:15-16; Jeremiah 1:5; Jonah 1:17; Matthew 6:26; Acts 12:7-11; Romans 13:1)!

How We Live Matters

Scripture presents us with a bit of a paradox. Though God is portrayed as being completely sovereign over our lives and the timing of death, Scripture also indicates that *how* we live can have something to do with *how long* we live.

On the one hand, it seems clear from Scripture that those who turn from God and perpetually live in sin can cut short their lives. First John 5:16 makes reference to the sin that leads to death. Apparently some Christians in the early church lost their lives as a result of perpetual and unrepentant sin (1 Corinthians 5:5; 11:29-32; Acts 5:1-11). In such cases, death may be viewed as God's ultimate discipline (see Hebrews 12:5-6). While their physical lives were lost, their souls remained saved and went to heaven.*

On the other hand, Scripture sets forth the general principle (not a promise) that those who honor God live long lives. Proverbs 10:27 tells us, "The fear of the LORD adds length to life, but the years of the wicked are cut short" (see also Deuteronomy 4:40; 2 Kings 20:1-6; Ephesians 6:2-3). The Book of Proverbs is brimming with verses on how yielding to godly wisdom can extend life. Such wisdom "will prolong your life many years" (3:2). Indeed, wisdom is portrayed as a woman, and "long life is in her right hand" (3:16). Follow wisdom, "and the years of your life will be many" (4:10). Through living according to godly wisdom "your days will be many, and years will be added to your life" (9:11). We are exhorted to remember that "the fear of the LORD is a fountain of life, turning a man from the snares of death" (14:27). So—*how we live does indeed matter!*

---

* Though theologians debate the issue, I believe Scripture teaches that all believers—even those who experience the "ultimate discipline"—are secure in salvation (see, for example, John 5:24; 6:35-37,39; 10:28-29).

Redeeming the Time

Our knowledge of our future in heaven should not be an end in itself. Rather, it should influence the way we live and how we use our time in the present.

I recently heard a speech in which a Christian leader said that the average 70-year-old man has spent a total of 24 years sleeping, 14 years working at a job, 8 years engaged in various amusements, 6 years sitting at the dinner table, 5 years in transportation, 4 years in conversation, 3 years in education, and 2 years in studying and reading. His other four years were spent in miscellaneous pursuits—except for the hour he spent every Sunday at church, as well as about five minutes per weekday engaged in prayer. This amounts to a tremendous total of five months that the average 70-year-old man gives to God over his life span. *Five months!*

A man by the name of Theodore Brennan once wrote a poem entitled "Those Wasted Years." In it, he portrayed the tragedy of a man who spent the majority of his life apart from a relationship with Christ:

> I looked upon a farm one day,
>> That once I used to own;
>>> The barn had fallen to the ground,
>>> The fields were overgrown.
>
> The house in which my children grew,
>> Where we had lived for years—
>>> I turned to see it broken down,
>>> And brushed aside the tears.
>
> I looked upon my soul one day,
>> To find it too had grown,

With thorns and nettles everywhere,
    The seeds neglect had sown.

The years had passed while I had cared
    for things of lesser worth;
      The things of Heaven I let go
        When minding things of Earth.

To Christ I turned with bitter tears,
    And cried, "O Lord, forgive!
      I haven't much time left for Thee,
        Not many years to live."

The wasted years forever gone,
    The days I can't recall;
      If I could live those days again,
        I'd make Him Lord of all.[18]

Wisdom calls us to redeem the time—*while there is yet time to redeem.* Theologian David Needham was surely right when he said:

> Out of all the eternal ages of our existence as God's children, these tiny years here on earth have a destiny that can never be repeated. The Bible tells us that in the stench of a sick and rotting world we are perfume bottles for the fragrance of Christ (2 Corinthians 2:15). In the gathering darkness we shine as stars (Philippians 2:15). If only we could grasp the awesome implications of these few years![19]

How about it? When you are 70 years old, will hindsight be kind or cruel to you? Will your life have been wasted because it had no real eternal significance? Will you shake your head as you look back on the ashes of a wasted life? Or will there be joy in your heart that results from a lifetime of heartfelt commitment to God?

Joni Eareckson Tada, the well-known quadriplegic, has contemplated such hard questions. With a caring heart, she urges, "Heaven may be as near as next year, or next week; so it makes good sense to spend some time here on earth thinking candid thoughts about that marvelous future reserved for us."[20] She then urges the heavenly minded Christian to make wise changes in life. In her thinking, the heavenly minded Christian invests wisely in relationships; seeks purity and honesty in conversations, goals, and motives; gives generously of time, money, and talent; and speaks the good news of Christ to people—all because such things involve eternal consequences and rewards.[21] I think she is right! We ought to do all these things while there is yet time to do them. After all, *our time will soon be past!*

As you read about the wonder of heaven in this book, may each page motivate you to wholly and unreservedly commit yourself to living for Christ, the divine Architect and Builder of the eternal city (see John 14:1-3). Live for Him daily. Serve Him with joy. Walk with Him in fellowship. Make Him the center of your life. You will find that to walk daily with Christ is to daily experience a little foretaste of heaven. And as you center your attention on heaven, you will be filled with hope during times of suffering. You'll recognize that this temporal world is not our true home, but rather we are "passing through" as pilgrims en route to a "better country"—a *heavenly* country, where our true treasure is (Philippians 3:20; see also Matthew 6:19-21).

1

ENTERING DEATH'S DOOR

The famed philosopher Diogenes was looking intently at a large collection of human bones piled one upon another. Alexander the Great stood nearby and became curious about what Diogenes was doing. When he asked the old man what he was doing, the reply was, "I am searching for the bones of your father, but I cannot seem to distinguish them from those of the slaves." Alexander got the point. *All are equal in death.*

Death has been called the great equalizer. It afflicts the young and the old, the weak and the strong, the king and the commoner, the rich and the poor, the educated and the ignorant, both male and female, and people of all colors. As the great Puritan preacher Jonathan Edwards (A.D. 1703–1758) put it, "Time cuts down all, both great and small."[1] J.C. Ryle (A.D. 1816–1900), Anglican bishop of Liverpool, likewise said that "we may die any day.... The youngest, the fairest, the strongest, the cleverest, all must go down one day before the scythe of the King of

Terrors."[2] Death has no favorites. All are equally victims of the grim reaper.

In this world of uncertainty, death is the one thing a person can really count on. From the moment of birth, human beings are on their steady way toward death. Pastor and theologian J. Sidlow Baxter (A.D. 1903–1999) lamented that "a million grave-yards proclaim with ceaseless voice that man is mortal and that the living are dying.... What is this revolving orb on which we live but the vast cemetery of mankind?"[3]

The current death rate among human beings is 100 percent. Current estimates are that over 90 million people die every year throughout the world. Randy Alcorn observes that "worldwide, three people die every second, 180 every minute, and nearly 11,000 every hour. If the Bible is right about what happens to us after death, it means that more than 250,000 people every day go either to Heaven or Hell."[4] If you are an average reader, then since the time you began reading this chapter, 305 people have died on planet Earth. Understandably, in view of the aging of America, with a steadily increasing percentage of the American public entering old age, the issue of death has become extremely relevant in this country.

Prior to the early twentieth century, most Americans died at about age 50 due to illness, and death normally occurred in the home. Typically the dying person's family would gather in the home, often at the person's bedside, and the person was helped to prepare for impending death.

By the middle of the twentieth century, however, death in America had become a more private matter. People did not want to openly discuss it anymore. Even though death is a universal experience, people did not want to think about it until absolutely compelled to.

In their attempt to avoid dealing with the issue head-on, people would often discuss things related to death and dying in disguised terms and clever euphemisms. Instead of saying someone died, people would say he or she was "laid to rest." Instead of making reference to the grave or the cemetery, people would speak of "perpetual family plots."

In their feeble attempt to defeat the grim reaper, some people have even paid so-called experts in the "science of cryonics" to take their freshly dead bodies, drain the blood, fill the body with freezer fluid, encase it in aluminum, and suspend it in a bath of liquid nitrogen. Far in the future, when a cure has been discovered for whatever disease caused the death, it is hoped that the body can be thawed and cured, and the person can resume living.[5] *Such folly!*

In recent years, Americans have become much more open in talking about death. It is no longer a taboo subject. After all, many Americans have reached an age in which they are confronting mortality—through the passing of a parent, the loss of a sibling or friend, or perhaps pains beneath their own breastbones.

In fact, Bill O'Reilly, of *The O'Reilly Factor*, says life after death has become big business today. "It is a huge business in America— books, tapes, lectures—and 65 percent of Americans say they do believe in an afterlife."[6]

Even though we are more willing to talk about death these days, however, our actions continue to indicate a powerful resistance toward the reality and finality of death. As Barry Morrow put it in his book *Heaven Observed: Glimpses of Transcendence in Everyday Life*, "We embalm our corpses, dress them up in new suits, pronounce last rites over them, and bury them in airtight caskets and concrete vaults in order to postpone the inevitable decay. Through our rituals we act out our stubborn reluctance to yield to this most powerful of human experiences."[7]

In recent days, it has become fashionable for some "experts" on death and dying to say that death is just a natural part of life. I beg to differ. Death is an *un*natural intruder, for God created human beings *to live*. It was only after the entrance of sin into the universe that death became a regular feature of earthly existence. One Christian leader suggests that the claim that death is a natural part of life is "like telling a quadriplegic that paralysis is a stage of exercise, or a divorcee that divorce is a stage of marriage. It's the kind of joke only a moron or a sadist would tell."[8]

By the way, I find it sobering to report to you that if you are an average reader, then since the time you began reading this chapter (assuming you are reading it in one sitting), 814 people have died on planet Earth.

What Happens at the Moment of Death?

Modern science tells us that death involves the cessation of all life (metabolic) processes.[9] Seen in such terms, death is strictly a physical, material event. It does not give recognition to the non-material (spiritual) part of humanity.

I once heard a sermon in which the preacher said,

> I remember talking to a medical student who just that morning had dissected his first human corpse. The body had been there in front of him on the bench and he had cut away different parts of the anatomy. It was like a lifeless wax model. He said to me, shaken a little from his first experience, "If this is all that we become at death, what is the point of anything?"[10]

From a biblical perspective, human beings are made up of both a material part (the physical body) *and* an immaterial part (the soul or spirit). When a human being physically dies, his or her immaterial part departs from the material body.

The New Testament concept of "death" (Greek: *thanatos*)

involves the idea of separation. More specifically, at the moment of death, a person's spirit or soul separates or departs from the body. This is why, when Stephen was being put to death by stoning, he prayed, "Lord Jesus, receive my spirit" (Acts 7:59). Verses such as this indicate that death for the believer involves his or her spirit departing from the physical body and immediately going into the presence of the Lord in heaven (see 2 Corinthians 5:8; Philippians 1:21-23). Death for the believer is thus an event that leads to a supremely blissful existence.

For the unbeliever, however, death holds grim prospects. Indeed, at death the immaterial part (soul or spirit) departs from the material body and goes not to heaven but to a place of horrific suffering (Luke 16:19-31) where they await the future judgment (2 Peter 2:9; Revelation 20:11-15).

Both believers and unbelievers remain in a disembodied state until the future day of resurrection. And what a glorious day that will be! God will reunite believers' spirits with their resurrected physical bodies (see Job 19:25-27; Psalm 49:15; Isaiah 26:19; John 6:39,40,44,54; 1 Corinthians 6:14; 1 Thessalonians 4:13-17; Revelation 20:4-6). These bodies will be specially suited to dwelling in heaven in the direct presence of God—the *perishable* will be made *imperishable* and the *mortal* will be made *immortal* (1 Corinthians 15:53). As one Christian scholar put it, believers "will exchange the temporal and imperfect for the eternal and perfect."[11] Unbelievers, too, will be resurrected, but they will spend eternity apart from God (Matthew 25:41,46; Revelation 20:13-15).

It is again sobering to report to you that if you are an average reader, and you are reading this chapter in one sitting, then since the time you began, 1202 people have died on planet Earth.

The Sin-Death Connection

In Scripture there is a direct connection between sin and death

(1 Chronicles 10:13; Proverbs 11:19; Ezekiel 18:4; Romans 5:12; 6:23). *One causes the other.* Death came into the universe because of sin. As noted previously, this means that death is not natural. It is an *un*natural intruder. God intended for human beings *to live.* Death is therefore something foreign and hostile to human life. Death has arisen because of our rebellion against God; it is a form of God's judgment.

But there is grace even in death. For death, as a judgment against sin, serves to prevent us from living forever in a state of sin. When Adam and Eve sinned in the Garden of Eden (Genesis 2:17; 3:19), God assigned an angel to guard the Tree of Life. This was to protect against Adam and Eve eating the Tree of Life while they were yet in a body of sin. How horrible it would be to live eternally in such a state.

By death, then, God graciously saw to it that every human being's existence in a state of sin had definite limits. And by sending a Savior into the world—the Lord Jesus Christ—God made salvation possible (Luke 2:11; John 3:17; 4:42; Acts 5:31; 1 Timothy 1:15; Hebrews 7:25). Those who believe in Him will live eternally at His side (John 3:15; 5:24; 11:25; 12:46; 20:31; Acts 16:31).

Man's Natural Fear of Death

In 2007 a film entitled *The Bucket List,* starring Jack Nicholson and Morgan Freeman, portrayed a road trip of two men who wanted to do the things they always said they would do before they "kicked the bucket." In an interview prior to the film's release, Nicholson was interviewed by *Parade* magazine. Reflecting on his personal life, Nicholson mused:

> I used to live so freely. The mantra for my generation
> was "Be your own man!" I always said, "Hey, you can
> have whatever rules you want—I'm going to have

mine. I'll accept the guilt. I'll pay the check. I'll do the
time." I chose my own way. That was my philosophi-
cal position well into my 50s. As I've gotten older, I've
had to adjust.

The reality of aging has been a wake-up call for Nicholson. He
represented the feelings of many without a Christian worldview
when he said: "We all want to go on forever, don't we? We fear the
unknown. Everybody goes to that wall, yet nobody knows what's
on the other side. That's why we fear death."[12]

Job aptly referred to death as the king of terrors (Job 18:14).
The psalmist said, "My heart is in anguish within me; the terrors of death assail me" (Psalm 55:4). The psalmist likewise
said, "The cords of death entangled me, the anguish of the grave
came upon me; I was overcome by trouble and sorrow" (Psalm
116:3). Hezekiah, a godly king of Judah, was grief-stricken
when he was informed of his impending death by Isaiah, and
he bitterly wept (2 Kings 20:1-11; see also Isaiah 38:10-13). Like
others, he was naturally fearful of death, and in a unique show
of grace, God extended his life another fifteen years. That was
a one-of-a-kind intervention on God's part, however. Hebrews
2:15 indicates that death has a long, long history of enslaving
people in fear.

Death is *the* great enemy of *all* human beings. Death strikes
down the good and the wicked, the strong and the weak. Without
any respect of persons, death carries its campaign of rampage and
destruction through whole communities and nations.

Unbelievers can find themselves faced with a nightmare of
nightmares at the prospect of death. Voltaire (1694–1778), a
French opponent of Christianity, found himself face-to-face with
his own death. He wrote, "I wish I had never been born." His
sense of desolation was so deep and chilling that toward the very

end, he implored his doctor, "I will give you half of what I am worth if you will give me six more months of life."[13]

There is something in each of us—*even Christians*—that shrinks back from the very mention of death. After all, God created us to live. Even the apostle Paul, a spiritual giant if there ever was one, considered death the "last enemy" to be conquered (1 Corinthians 15:26-27; see also Isaiah 25:8).

Except for those living Christians who will be instantly transformed into their resurrection bodies at the future Rapture,* *all* Christians will eventually go through death's door. There will come a time when each of our spirits will depart from the body. In some cases, death will be near-instant (as in a car wreck). In other cases, the process of death may be long and drawn out (as in some cases involving cancer).

If we're honest, most of us would admit that we've thought about what death might be like for each of us. In her interesting book *Heaven: Your Real Home,* Joni Eareckson Tada reflects:

> I look at my own degenerating body and wonder how I will approach that final passage. Will it be short and sweet? Or long and agonizing? Will my husband be able to take care of me? Or will my quadriplegia better suit me for a nursing home? It's not so much I'm afraid of *death* as *dying*.[14]

Thankfully, regardless of the actual *process* of dying, the prospect of heaven does much to reduce the Christian's fear of death itself. As Anne Graham Lotz (daughter of evangelist Billy Graham) put it, "The prospect of death can fill you and me with terror and

---

* The "Rapture" is that event immediately prior to the beginning of the future Tribulation period when believers will be physically snatched off the earth by Christ. At that time living believers will instantly (in the blink of an eye) receive their glorified resurrection bodies. See 1 Thessalonians 4:13-17 and 1 Corinthians 15:51-52.

dread—*unless we know where we are going.*"[15] Her words reflect
the apostle Paul's teaching that because of what Jesus has done for
us, the sting has been taken out of death (1 Corinthians 15:55-56;
see also 1 Thessalonians 4:13-18). Bible scholars tell us that Paul
was alluding to the lethal and excruciatingly painful sting of a
scorpion. This is metaphorically what death is like. The good news
is that Christ, in His resurrection from the dead, extracted death's
stinger and robbed the grave of its triumph.[16]

Because of what Christ accomplished at the cross, and His
subsequent resurrection from the dead, we need never be terror-
ized by death's ever-present threat again. Because He is risen, we
too shall rise. Our destiny is heaven!

For the Christian, then, physical death is actually a step into
life. It is not a *terminus,* but a *transition* into great glory, a glory
that has been revealed by God. The apostle Paul wrote, "As it is
written: 'No eye has seen, no ear has heard, no mind has conceived what God has prepared for those who love him'—*but God
has revealed it to us by his Spirit*" (1 Corinthians 2:9-10, emphasis
added). These wondrous things about heaven and the afterlife that
were once unknown to humankind (especially in Old Testament
times) were now revealed by the Holy Spirit to God's apostles
and are recorded in the pages of holy Scripture for us. And what
Scripture reveals about heaven and the afterlife is truly astounding. The greater part of this book will seek to expound on these
splendorous revelations.

In view of the above, even though 2800 people have died since
the time you began reading this chapter (assuming you read it
in one sitting), we as Christians need not fear passing through
the valley of the shadow of death (Psalm 23:4). Our Lord is with
us during life, and He will meet us face-to-face at the moment
of death (Philippians 1:21-23; 2 Corinthians 5:8). *It is an event to
anticipate with joy.*

2

BIBLICAL PORTRAYALS
OF DEATH

F rench philosopher Francois Rabelais (A.D. 1494–1553), upon
his deathbed, said, "I am going to the great Perhaps."[1] Unlike
the uncertain view of Rabelais, and others like him who hold to a
non-Christian worldview, the Bible is quite clear about what we
can expect beyond death's door. In fact, death is described in a
rich variety of ways in the Bible. By viewing death from a number
of different biblical vantage points, we are enabled to understand
a great deal about this mysterious event.

The Way of All the Earth

Sometimes the Bible refers to death as "the way of all the
earth," emphasizing the universality of the death experience. We
read, "When the time drew near for David to die, he gave a charge
to Solomon his son. 'I am about to go the way of all the earth,' he

said. 'So be strong, show yourself a man'" (1 Kings 2:1-2). Joshua spoke of his death in similar fashion: "Now I am about to go the way of all the earth..." (Joshua 23:14; see also Job 30:23).

Death is "the way of all the earth" in that it is the path trodden by all human beings. No one is exempt. One day, should the Lord tarry in His coming, you and I will go "the way of all the earth." The moment our physical bodies keel over, however, our spirits immediately depart the body and go into the direct presence of Jesus Christ in heaven (Philippians 1:21; 2 Corinthians 5:8). And, gloriously, our spirits will one day be reunited with permanent resurrection bodies that will never again go "the way of all the earth"! (see 1 Corinthians 15).

The Journey of No Return

Job spoke of his eventual death this way: "Only a few years will pass before I go on the journey of no return" (Job 16:22; see also 7:9; 10:21; 2 Samuel 12:23). Such words remind us of the permanence of passing from mortal life. Once we pass through death's door, we have forever left mortal life (Hebrews 9:27). And this short life on earth is the only time we have to decide for or against Christ. This is why Scripture urges, "Now is the day of salvation" (2 Corinthians 6:2). Once we die, there is no further time—no further opportunity (or second chance)—to believe in Jesus for salvation so that we can spend an eternity in heaven.

Being Gathered to One's People

When the Lord spoke to Moses about the impending death of Aaron, He said, "Aaron will be *gathered to his people*. He will not enter the land I give the Israelites...Get Aaron and his son Eleazar and take them up Mount Hor. Remove Aaron's garments and put them on his son Eleazar, for Aaron will be *gathered to his people*; he will die there" (Numbers 20:24-26, emphasis added).

We read the same about Ishmael: "Altogether, Ishmael lived a hundred and thirty-seven years. He breathed his last and died, and he was *gathered to his people*" (Genesis 25:17, emphasis added; see also Genesis 35:29; 49:29,33; Numbers 27:13; 31:2; Deuteronomy 32:50; Judges 2:10). Bible scholar Arnold Fruchtenbaum draws our attention to the order of events in Ishmael's case: "Notice that first, physical death takes place, Ishmael dies; then after death, he is seen as *gathered unto his people,* as joining a company that preceded him or that had gone on in advance."[2]

Such verses portray death as a universal experience. Like all of their ancestors before them, Aaron and Ishmael died and joined all of them in death. You and I will one day be gathered to *our* people—that is, Christians in heaven (see 1 Thessalonians 4:13-17; Revelation 7:9).

Breathing One's Last

Death is sometimes described in the Bible as "breathing one's last." We read that "Ishmael lived a hundred and thirty-seven years. He breathed his last and died, and he was gathered to his people" (Genesis 25:17). Similarly, "when Jacob had finished giving instructions to his sons, he drew his feet up into the bed, breathed his last and was gathered to his people" (Genesis 49:33). Job reflected that "man dies and is laid low; he breathes his last and is no more" (Job 14:10).

This description of death focuses solely on the cessation of life in the physical body. We learn from other Scriptures that once a Christian "breathes his last," his spirit departs the body and immediately goes into God's presence (2 Corinthians 5:8; Philippians 1:21-23).

A Withering Away

Death is occasionally described as a "withering away." Man

"springs up like a flower and withers away; like a fleeting shadow, he does not endure" (Job 14:2). The flower fades. Its beauty quickly vanishes. The shadow is likewise fleeting, for it too fades. And so it is with human life (see 1 Chronicles 29:15; Job 8:9; Psalm 102:11; 144:4).

The psalmist said to God, "You sweep men away in the sleep of death; they are like the new grass of the morning—though in the morning it springs up new, by evening it is dry and withered" (Psalm 90:5-6). Of course, this speaks only about the cessation of life in the physical body. One's spirit certainly does not "wither away."

Departing the Body

The great apostle Paul said, "If I am to go on living in the body, this will mean fruitful labor for me. Yet what shall I choose? I do not know! I am torn between the two: I desire to *depart and be with Christ,* which is better by far" (Philippians 1:22-23, emphasis added; see also 2 Corinthians 5:8). Paul considered departure from earthly life and into the Lord's presence something to be desired—it is *better by far.*[3] Theologian Wayne Grudem comments: "Death is a temporary cessation of bodily life and a separation of the soul from the body. Once a believer has died, though his or her physical body remains on the earth and is buried, at the moment of death the soul (or spirit) of that believer goes immediately into the presence of God with rejoicing."[4] This is precisely what Paul knew would happen upon his death: "To the Apostle Paul, death was not a darksome passageway, where all our treasures rot away in a swift corruption; it was a place of gracious transition, 'a covered way that leadeth into light.'"[5] It was thus not something to be feared.

When it finally came time for Paul's death, he said, "I am already being poured out like a drink offering, and the time has come for my departure" (2 Timothy 4:6). Paul was drawing on Old Testament imagery in this verse. In Old Testament days wine was poured around the base of the altar as an offering (Numbers 15:1-12; 28:7,24). Paul thus viewed his own impending death—his "departure"—as an offering poured out to Christ.

Dismissal from Earthly Life

Recognizing that God alone is sovereign over the timing and circumstances of death, Simeon, after beholding the Christ-child as God had promised, said, "Sovereign Lord, as you have promised, you now dismiss your servant in peace" (Luke 2:29). In death God sovereignly dismisses one from earthly life, at which time he or she enters the afterlife (see also Luke 12:20).

Scripture consistently portrays God as being absolutely sovereign. He rules the universe, controls all things, and is Lord over all (see Ephesians 1). There is nothing that can happen in this universe that is beyond the reach of His control. All forms of existence are within the scope of His absolute dominion. Psalm 66:7 affirms that "he rules forever by his power." God asserts, "My purpose will stand, and I will do all that I please" (Isaiah 46:10). God assures us, "Surely, as I have planned, so it will be, and as I have purposed, so it will stand" (Isaiah 14:24). Proverbs 16:9 tells us, "In his heart a man plans his course, but the Lord determines his steps." Proverbs 19:21 says, "Many are the plans in a man's heart, but it is the Lord's purpose that prevails." Consistent with such verses is the fact that God sovereignly dismisses human beings from earthly life, at which time they enter the afterlife.

Some, however, have wondered how God's sovereignty over death relates to earthly causes of death. It is important to recognize that even though there may be immediate "earthly" causes of death—such as a disease, a gunshot wound, a car wreck, or the like—still, it is God who is sovereign over death.

The death of Saul in the Old Testament illustrates this truth. First Chronicles 10:1-4 tells us that the immediate cause of Saul's death was the enemy's arrows and his own sword. But several verses later, we read, "Saul died because he was unfaithful to the LORD; he did not keep the word of the LORD, and even consulted a medium for guidance, and did not inquire of the LORD. So *the LORD put him to death* and turned the kingdom over to David son of Jesse" (1 Chronicles 10:13-14, emphasis added). Despite the immediate circumstances that brought death for Saul (enemy arrows and his own sword), God was nevertheless sovereignly behind those circumstances.

Earthly Tent Being Destroyed

Tents were popular "homes" in biblical times, particularly among shepherds who had to move sheep and goats around, and farmers who needed to be near their crops for part of the year. Abraham and his descendants lived in tents for hundreds of years (see Genesis 12:8). These tents were generally made from goat hair. The material of the tent was supported by poles, which were about six feet high in the middle, with the outer poles being shorter. Such tents were extremely flimsy and weak structures. It did not take much to knock them down.

With this backdrop in mind, the apostle Paul—himself a tent maker (Acts 18:3)—graphically described death as an earthly tent being destroyed: "Now we know that if the earthly tent we live in is destroyed, we have a building from God, an eternal house in heaven, not built by human hands" (2 Corinthians 5:1). Our present bodies, Paul said, are but temporary and flimsy abodes. They are weak, frail, and vulnerable. We "camp" in these "tents" during our journey toward heaven. Our earthly bodies, in their present mortal state, are not designed to be lasting habitations.

The same was true even of Jesus, for when Jesus was born

as a human being, Scripture tells us that He "lived [more literally: *tabernacled* or *tented*] among us" (John 1:14). But Scripture
tells us that, following death, He was gloriously resurrected in a
permanent body (Matthew 28:6-7; Luke 24:39; Acts 1:3; 1 Corinthians 15; Revelation 1:5).

The good news is that a time will one day come when each of our
flimsy "habitations" will also be resurrected (John 6:39-40,44,54;
1 Corinthians 6:14; 1 Thessalonians 4:13-17; Revelation 20:4-6),
and our resurrection bodies will be permanent and indestructible,
just like Jesus' (1 John 3:2). That is a day to look forward to.

Entering Paradise

Jesus spoke of death in terms of entering into paradise. To one
of the thieves being crucified with Him, He said, "I tell you the
truth, today you will be with me in paradise" (Luke 23:43).

Paradise is a place of incredible bliss and serene rest in the very
presence of God (2 Corinthians 12:2). The apostle Paul himself
was "caught up" to paradise. Indeed, as one Christian scholar put
it, "Paul was raptured ('caught up' is from the same verb *harpazō*
used in 1 Thes. 4:17 of saints at the Rapture) to the third heaven,
the dwelling place of Christ and the saints, which Jesus called
paradise (Luke 23:43; cf. Rev. 2:7)."[6] What Paul witnessed there
led to his unflinching conviction that "our light and momentary
troubles are achieving for us an eternal glory that far outweighs
them all" (2 Corinthians 4:17). We therefore need not fear death.

The Physical Body "Sleeps"

Death is often described in the Bible as "sleep," for the body
takes on the *appearance* of sleep. This is what Jesus was talking
about when He said to the disciples, "Our friend Lazarus has fallen
asleep; but I am going there to wake him up." His disciples replied,
"Lord, if he sleeps, he will get better." The disciples thought Jesus

meant natural sleep, but He was talking about death. So Jesus told them plainly, "Lazarus is dead" (John 11:11-14).

Like Lazarus, the Old Testament King David "fell asleep" in death. When David "had served God's purpose in his own generation, he fell asleep; he was buried with his fathers and his body decayed" (Acts 13:36).

Similarly, when Stephen was being stoned to death, he prayed, "'Lord Jesus, receive my spirit.' Then he fell on his knees and cried out, 'Lord, do not hold this sin against them.' When he had said this, he fell asleep" (Acts 7:59-60).

It is critical to keep in mind that the reference to "sleep" pertains *only* to the physical body and not to the soul. The soul does not sleep, for it remains fully conscious. The believer's soul in the afterlife is fully awake and active in the presence of God, even carrying on conversations (see Revelation 6:9-11). The unbeliever's soul is also fully conscious in a place of great suffering (Luke 16:19-31).

The Believer's Response to Death

When Martin Luther's daughter, Magdalena, was 14 years old, she was taken sick and lay dying. Luther prayed, "O God, I love her so, but nevertheless, Thy will be done."

Then he turned to his daughter and said, "Magdalena, would you rather be with me, or would you rather go and be with your Father in heaven?"

The girl said, "Father, as God wills."

Luther held her in his arms as she passed away. And as they laid her to rest, he said, "Oh my dear Magdalena, you will rise and shine like the stars and the sun. How strange to be so sorrowful and yet to know that all is at peace, that all is well."

Death is still a great enemy. As we have noted earlier, however, Christ has taken the sting out of death for the Christian

(1 Corinthians 15:55). Luther could thus rest in Christ during this difficult time because he knew he would be reunited with his daughter (see 1 Thessalonians 4:13-17; see also 2 Samuel 12:23).

As we look at the lives of other great saints, we see a pattern emerge. Indeed, in each case we find saints facing death not with terror or dread, as unbelievers do, but with a calm and blessed assurance that all is well—that soon the dying one would be in the direct presence of the blessed Lord.

- Missionary David Brainerd, on his deathbed, said, "I am going into eternity, and it is sweet for me to think of eternity."

- John Wesley, on his deathbed, said, "The best of all is, God is with us. Farewell! Farewell!"

- Susanna Wesley, on her deathbed, said, "Children, when I am gone, sing a song of praise to God."

- Lady Glenorchy, on her deathbed, said, "If this is dying, it is the pleasantest thing imaginable."

- Pastor John Pawson, on his deathbed, said, "I know I am dying, but my deathbed is a bed of roses. I have no thorns planted upon my dying pillow. Heaven is already begun."[7]

Death Should Affect the Way We Live

What people believe about death tends to greatly influence how they conduct their lives. We live to a great extent in the steady consciousness that we are one day going to die. This is why the psalmist prayed to God: "Teach us to number our days aright, that we may gain a heart of wisdom" (Psalm 90:12). He also prayed, "Show me, O Lord, my life's end and the number of my days; let me know how fleeting is my life" (Psalm 39:4). Especially as we pass middle age and head on into our "senior" years, we become increasingly aware that our time is winding down. What is crucial to grasp is that no matter what age we are, our understanding of death—and what lies beyond it—has everything to do with our understanding of life and its meaning.

Perhaps this is one of the most important and practical aspects of the book you are reading. Let us never forget that the Bible talks about death so that it can instruct us about life and teach us how to have an eternal perspective during our brief time on earth. The reality of impending death serves to detach our interest from the things of this temporal, passing world and centers our attention on the afterlife.[8] Put another way, death helps us to become more heavenly minded.

In recognition that death would one day visit, Jonathan Edwards sought to keep his Puritan habit of framing spiritual resolutions to discipline himself throughout life. George Marsden, author of the wonderful book *Jonathan Edwards: A Life,* tells us that "in a number of them he reminded himself, as he had been taught since childhood, to think of his own dying—or to live as though—he had only an hour left before his death or 'before I should hear the last trump.'"[9] Edwards commented that "it becomes us to spend this life only as a journey toward heaven… to which we should subordinate all other concerns of life. Why should we labor for or set our hearts on anything else, but that which is our proper end and true happiness?"[10] He thus made—and sought to *keep*—the following (among other) resolutions:

- "Resolved, to endeavor to obtain for myself as much happiness, in the other world, as I possibly can."

- "Resolved, that I will live so as I shall wish I had done when I come to die."

- "Resolved, to endeavor to my utmost to act as I can think I should do, if I had already seen the happiness of heaven, and hell's torments."[11]

One resolution I suggest we all consider involves often reminding ourselves that life on earth is short and the afterlife is long. So it makes good sense to ensure a destiny of heaven for the afterlife. As J. Sidlow Baxter put it in his book *The Other Side of Death*, "However big and pressing the questions related to our present short life on earth may seem, they shrink into littleness compared with this timeless, measureless concern of death and the vast hereafter. How long earthly life looks to questing youth! How quickly fled it seems to the aged!"[12] Let the wise resolve to remind themselves often of the brevity of earthly life!

Developing an Eternal Perspective

Our true significance comes not from the accumulation of status and earthly wealth, but from our relationship with Jesus Christ. After all, we will not take our earthly wealth or status with us into the next life. How strange, then, that so many today focus so much of their energies on building up that which will perish. Modern man, for the most part, has failed in maintaining an eternal perspective.

Do you remember the first and last names of your maternal grandmother? Perhaps you do. But many do not.

Do you remember the first and last names of your great grandmother? How about your great great grandmother? Or your great great great grandmother?

If you are like most people, you do not remember the names of those beyond your grandmother. As it is with your great grandmother (and beyond), so it will one day be with you. Just a few generations after you die, people in your own family will likely not even remember your name. For all practical purposes in their lives, it will be as though you never existed. Regardless of whether you attain high status and great wealth, you, like most others, will not be remembered.

I say this not to depress you; I am simply emphasizing the ultimate futility of spending all our efforts building status and wealth for this life. The things of this earth are temporal and will pass. When you enter the next life, you will leave behind *all* your earthly goods.

How much better it is to focus on eternity, recognizing that our only true significance lies in a personal relationship with Jesus Christ (Philippians 3:7-8). Jesus urged His followers, "Store up for yourselves treasures in heaven, where moth and rust do not destroy, and where thieves do not break in and steal" (Matthew 6:20). Such words call us to examine our lives and our priorities. Such words require an eternal perspective. With this eternal perspective in mind, the apostle Paul urged Christians, "Set your hearts on things above, where Christ is seated at the right hand of God. Set your minds on things above, not on earthly things" (Colossians 3:1-2).

Many of us are familiar with the pessimistic statement made by the author of the Book of Ecclesiastes: "The day of death [is] better than the day of birth" (Ecclesiastes 7:1). Bible expositor John MacArthur is correct in stating that the author's intention was to be cynical about the meaninglessness and futility of this earthly life. However, as MacArthur also notes, "There is a valid sense for the Christian in which it is *true* that our death ushers us into an infinitely greater glory than our birth ever did. The confidence that heaven awaits us should fill us with a glorious hope."[13] Because of this glorious hope, we can adopt the apostle Paul's attitude as our own: "For to me, to live is Christ and to die is gain" (Philippians 1:21).

3

LIFE IN THE
INTERMEDIATE STATE

I love the true story evangelist Billy Graham tells about his maternal grandmother. He said that when she died, the whole room seemed to fill with a heavenly light. "She sat up in bed and almost laughingly said, 'I see Jesus. He has His arms outstretched toward me. I see Ben [her husband who had died some years earlier] and I see the angels.' She slumped over, absent from the body but present with the Lord."[1] Ultimately, the death of a Christian is not a loss. It is a lasting, perpetual gain. For Scripture assures us that the moment Christians die, their spirits depart from their physical bodies and go immediately into the presence of God in heaven.

Some people have wrongly assumed that upon the moment of death and subsequent entrance into heaven, people instantly receive their permanent resurrection bodies. This is not the view of Scripture, however. Scripture consistently portrays the day of resurrection as yet future, and those who are presently dead do not yet have their resurrection bodies. They await the future resurrection with great anticipation.

The state of our existence between physical death and the future resurrection is properly called the "intermediate state." It is an *in-between* state—that is, it is the state of our existence *in-between* the time our mortal bodies die and the time we receive permanent resurrection bodies in the future.

People debate, however, over the temporary state of Christians who die: Do they exist in a disembodied state in heaven, or might they have a temporary body that will one day be replaced with a permanent resurrection body? Let's take a brief look at the views of Christians on both sides of the issue:

The Temporary Body View

Some Christians believe that at death, the Christian in heaven receives a temporary body. They appeal to 2 Corinthians 5:1-4, which they interpret as saying that once our earthly bodies (*tents*) die, we immediately receive new temporary bodies (*buildings*) in heaven.[2] We are told that such temporary bodies might be analogous to the human-looking bodies that angels sometimes appear in when visiting earth. As one Christian expositor puts it, "Given the consistent physical descriptions of the intermediate Heaven and those who dwell there, it seems possible—though this is certainly debatable—that between our earthly life and our bodily resurrection, God may grant us some physical form that will allow us to function as human beings while in that unnatural state 'between bodies,' awaiting our resurrection."[3]

Supporters of this view also point to the fact that the Christian martyrs of Revelation 6:9-11 are portrayed as wearing white robes. Moreover, Luke 16:19-31 portrays an unbeliever who had died (the rich man) wanting his "tongue" to be cooled by Lazarus's "finger" dipped in water. Such imagery, it is suggested, might indicate the presence of a temporary body in the intermediate state. Then, on that future resurrection day, believers will receive their permanent resurrection bodies (1 Corinthians 15:12-32).

The Disembodied Spirit View

Other Christians believe that we exist as disembodied spirits in the intermediate state. They hold that the body mentioned in 2 Corinthians 5:1-4 (a "building") cannot be viewed as a temporary body, for it is referred to as "an *eternal* house in heaven" in verse 1 (emphasis added). Hence, this refers not to a temporary body but to the permanent (*eternal*) resurrection body that we will eventually receive from God.[4]

Further, the context itself indicates that we will be "naked" or bodiless during the intermediate state. As scholar Arnold Fruchtenbaum notes, "Verses 3-4 do imply that there will be a temporary period of nakedness for the soul until it is clothed with the resurrection body. The implication is that in the intermediate state, there is no intermediate body. The believer is unclothed; he is naked; he has no body until he receives his resurrection body."[5]

Of course, the backdrop to all this is the scriptural emphasis that human beings have both a material part and an immaterial part. The material part of a human being is the body (see Genesis 2:7; 3:19). The immaterial part is the soul or spirit (these terms are used interchangeably in Scripture).

At death, a human being becomes disembodied when his or her spirit or soul *departs* from the physical body (see Genesis 35:18; 2 Corinthians 5:8; Philippians 1:21-23; Revelation 6:9-10). This is what happened to Billy Graham's maternal grandmother. At the moment of death, her spirit departed from her physical body and went to be with Jesus in heaven. Her body was buried in a grave a few days later.

Many verses in Scripture speak of the "departure" of the spirit at death:

- The preacher tells us that at the moment of death "the spirit returns to God who gave it" (Ecclesiastes 12:7).

- At the moment of Jesus' death, He prayed to the Father: "Into your hands I commit my spirit" (Luke 23:46). Jesus was here committing His human immaterial soul or spirit to the Father. And since Christ was not raised from the dead until three days after His crucifixion, we must conclude that Jesus' human soul or spirit went directly to the Father's presence in heaven while His body laid in the tomb.[6]

- When Stephen was dying after being stoned, he prayed, "Lord Jesus, receive my spirit" (Acts 7:59). Stephen was clearly asking Jesus to receive his soul or spirit, the part of him that would survive the death of his physical body.

- In 2 Corinthians 5:8 the apostle Paul affirmed: "We are confident, I say, and would prefer to be *away from the body* and *at home with the Lord*" (emphasis added). J. Sidlow Baxter, in his book *The Other Side of Death*, observes, "Notice, he does not say that to be absent from this body is to be clothed with that body; but he does say that to be absent from this body is to be 'present with the Lord.' Clearly, there is an intermediate state during which we are temporarily bodiless."[7]

- In Revelation 6:9-10 we read about the souls of Christians who will be bodily slain during the future

Tribulation period.[8] These souls are said to be under God's altar, and they are portrayed as speaking with God, even though their dead physical bodies were still on earth. It is true that they are said to be clothed in white robes, but because so much of the Book of Revelation is symbolic in nature, it may be that the white robes merely symbolize that these believers are in heaven because they have been made holy (white, or purified) by the death of Christ on their behalf.

In this view, then, Christians who depart earthly life exist as disembodied spirits in the presence of God, and their existence is joyful and blissful. As Baxter puts it, "Although, as yet, they are not 'clothed upon' with the promised resurrection bodies, their present state is one of exquisite fellowship with Christ; of ineffable felicity and surpassing joy. They know why Paul wrote, 'I have a desire to depart and to be with Christ, which is far better.'"[9]

This separation of the spirit from the physical body is only a temporary situation. The Scriptures indicate that there is a day coming in which God will reunite each person's soul or spirit to his or her resurrection body (Job 19:25-27; Psalm 49:15; Isaiah 26:19; John 6:39-40,44,54; 1 Corinthians 6:14; 1 Thessalonians 4:13-17; Revelation 20:4-6). When that day finally arrives, human beings will never again be in a situation where they are disembodied. They will live forever in their resurrection bodies.

Resurrected believers will live forever in the immediate presence of God (2 Corinthians 5:8; Philippians 1:21-23; 1 Thessalonians 4:13-17). Resurrected unbelievers will spend eternity in a place of great suffering called the lake of fire (Revelation 20:15; 21:8). This sobering reality was portrayed at an Indiana cemetery that has a tombstone over a hundred years old. This tombstone bears the following epitaph:

> Pause, stranger, when you pass me by;
>> As you are now, so once was I.
> As I am now, so you will be,
>> So prepare for death and follow me.

An unknown passerby had read those words and scratched this reply below them:

> To follow you I'm not content,
>> Until I know which way you went.[10]

The passerby was right. The important thing about death is what *follows* death. Where are *you* going?

Conscious Awareness in the Intermediate State

A number of people throughout church history have wrongly concluded that at the moment of death, consciousness vanishes. They think the soul "sleeps." This is not the view of Scripture, however. The Scriptures never speak of the soul sleeping; instead, they speak of the body sleeping. This is because the body takes on the appearance of sleep at the moment of death.

When we examine the Scriptures, we clearly see that the human soul or spirit is always portrayed as being fully conscious in the intermediate state (see Revelation 6:9-10). This is best illustrated in the story Jesus told of the rich man and Lazarus:

> There was a rich man who was dressed in purple and fine linen and lived in luxury every day. At his gate was laid a beggar named Lazarus, covered with sores and longing to eat what fell from the rich man's table. Even the dogs came and licked his sores.
>
> The time came when the beggar died and the angels carried him to Abraham's side. The rich man also died and was buried. In hell, where he was in torment, he

looked up and saw Abraham far away, with Lazarus by his side. So he called to him, "Father Abraham, have pity on me and send Lazarus to dip the tip of his finger in water and cool my tongue, because I am in agony in this fire."

But Abraham replied, "Son, remember that in your lifetime you received your good things, while Lazarus received bad things, but now he is comforted here and you are in agony. And besides all this, between us and you a great chasm has been fixed, so that those who want to go from here to you cannot, nor can anyone cross over from there to us."

He answered, "Then I beg you, father, send Lazarus to my father's house, for I have five brothers. Let him warn them, so that they will not also come to this place of torment."

Abraham replied, "They have Moses and the Prophets; let them listen to them."

"No, father Abraham," he said, "but if someone from the dead goes to them, they will repent."

He said to him, "If they do not listen to Moses and the Prophets, they will not be convinced even if someone rises from the dead" (Luke 16:19-31).

Such words surely indicate that both Christians and non-Christians are in a state of consciousness in the intermediate state, fully aware of all that is transpiring around them. They are also in complete possession of their memory, and even think about their loved ones still alive on earth.

In terms of the wicked dead (unbelievers), Jesus' story indicates that no one can comfort them, they cannot leave the place of torment, and they are entirely responsible for not having listened in time to the warnings of Scripture. This is why Scripture admonishes people who are still alive on earth that, "now is the day of salvation" (2 Corinthians 6:2). Sadly, many fail to heed this admonition and die before trusting in Christ.

Another passage that points to conscious existence in the intermediate state is Matthew 17:1-8. In this passage Jesus, along with Peter, James, and John, is portrayed as being on a high mountain. Jesus was then transfigured before them, and His face became as bright as the sun. At that moment, both Moses and Elijah—whose time on earth had long passed—supernaturally appeared to Jesus from the intermediate state and spoke with Him.[11] Notice that they were fully conscious and carried on a conversation with Jesus. So it is with all of us who die. We are fully conscious and we can converse with others who are with us.

The Intermediate State Prior to Christ's First Coming: Two Views

By now I am sure you are beginning to pick up on the fact that when it comes to the intermediate state, Christians do have some different opinions. This is certainly true in regard to the intermediate state *prior to Christ's first coming*—that is, the intermediate state in Old Testament times. The two views Christians have held on this matter might be categorized as the Hades view and the Heaven view. Let us briefly consider these.

The Hades View

According to this view, there were two compartments in Hades (the realm of the dead[12])—one for the saved and another for the unsaved. They were separated by a "great gulf" which no man could pass (Luke 16:26 KJV). The saved would be in "Abraham's bosom." The section for the unsaved was called "torments" (see Luke 16:23 KJV).

This view holds that when Christ (described in 1 Corinthians 15:20 as the "firstfruits" of the resurrection), ascended, He led these Old Testament saints from Abraham's bosom into heaven with Him for the first time.[13] Proponents of this view believe that Ephesians 4:8 may relate to this Christ-led transfer: "When he ascended on high, he led captives in his train and gave gifts to men." Some people also think that Revelation 1:18 may relate to this event, since Christ is portrayed as the One who holds "the keys of death and Hades." Christ is said to have "unlocked" Hades for the righteous dead (Old Testament believers) and took them to heaven.

The Heaven View

Contrary to the Hades view, this view (my view) holds that the souls of Old Testament believers went directly to heaven the moment they died. For example, the psalmist believed he would be directly in the presence of God upon the moment of death, finding pleasure and fullness of joy in His presence (Psalm 16:10-11). Moreover, God took Enoch to be with Himself in heaven (Genesis 5:24; see also Hebrews 11:5), and Elijah was caught up into heaven when he departed (2 Kings 2:1). Theologian Charles Ryrie thus asks, "Are we to understand that Elijah was taken at his translation to Sheol/Hades and not heaven? I think not; rather, the Old Testament saint went immediately to heaven to wait for the resurrection of his body at the second coming of Christ."[14]

We also note David's assurance of going to heaven upon the moment of death. In the classic Psalm 23, David reflected, "Surely goodness and love will follow me all the days of my life, and *I will dwell in the house of the LORD forever*" (verse 6, emphasis added). Bible expositor John MacArthur offers this helpful insight:

David was certain that once his life was over, he would dwell in the house of the Lord forever (which can refer only to heaven). Notice that he goes immediately from "all the days of my life" to "dwell[ing] in the house of the Lord." The hope he expresses here is exactly the same as Paul's: "to be absent from the body and to be at home with the Lord" (2 Cor. 5:8 NASB).[15]

In keeping with this, when Moses and Elijah (who had long departed earthly life) appeared to Christ on the Mount of Transfiguration (Matthew 17:3), they apparently appeared directly from heaven. It seems clear that their habitat had not been some intermediate compartment of Hades.[16]

In this view, Abraham's "bosom" (Luke 16:23 KJV) is a metaphorical description of heaven. It is the place to which Abraham went, which apparently is equated with the "kingdom of heaven" (Matthew 8:11). Ryrie observes that "Abraham's bosom is not said to be in Hades but rather 'far away' from it. Abraham's bosom is a figurative phrase for paradise, or the presence of God. It was paradise that was promised to the repentant thief by the Lord (Luke 23:43), not a blissful compartment of Hades."[17]

Finally, this view holds that when Christ "led captivity captive" (Ephesians 4:8 KJV), He was not leading friends into heaven, but rather bringing foes into bondage. It is a reference to His conquering the forces of evil. After all, Christians could never be considered "captives" in Abraham's bosom. We get to heaven by our own free choice (see Matthew 23:37; 2 Peter 3:9). So even though a number of highly respected theologians have held to the Hades view, I believe the Heaven view is most consistent with Scripture.[18]

What Is the Intermediate State Like for Christians?

We read in 2 Corinthians 12:2 that the apostle Paul was "caught up to the third heaven," also called "paradise" (verse 4).

While there, Paul heard inexpressible things that he was prohibited from revealing. Apparently heaven is so incredible—so resplendently glorious, so ineffable—that God, for His own reasons, forbade Paul to reveal to mortals on earth what lay ahead in heaven. But we do find some nuggets of gold scattered throughout Scripture that give us a foretaste of this wonderful future habitat for Christians.

With Christ in Heaven

First and foremost, Christians are in continuous fellowship with Christ in the intermediate state. This is evident in numerous passages. Jesus told the thief on the cross, "I tell you the truth, today you will be with me in paradise" (Luke 23:43). While being stoned to death, Stephen prayed, "Lord Jesus, receive my spirit" (Acts 7:59). The apostle Paul said, "I desire to depart and be with Christ, which is better by far" (Philippians 1:23; see also Revelation 6:9-10).

It is interesting to note that in Philippians 1, when Paul said he desired to "depart" and be with Christ, the word "depart" was used in biblical times in reference to a ship being loosed from its moorings (devices meant to secure the ship) to sail away from the dock. The "mooring" that kept Paul from departing to heaven was his commitment to work among believers on earth until his work was complete. His ultimate desire, however, was to "sail" directly into God's presence.[19]

The word "depart" was also used in biblical times for freeing someone from chains. Here on earth, you and I are anchored to the hardships and heartaches of this life. In death, however, these chains are broken. We are set free for entry into heaven. At the moment of death, the spirit departs the physical body and goes directly into the presence of the Lord.

Note that this verse is *not* speaking of a future resurrection at which time Paul will be with Christ. Rather, Paul is saying that the very moment after physical death occurs, his spirit or soul will be with Christ. How do we know this? It is clear from the Greek text! Without going into excessive detail, suffice it to say that the phrases "to depart" and "to be with Christ" are, in the Greek, two sides of one coin, indicating that the *very moment* after Paul "departs" the body at death, he will be with Christ in heaven.[20]

Along these same lines, the apostle Paul said: "Therefore we are always confident and know that as long as we are at home in the body we are away from the Lord.... We are confident, I say, and would prefer to be away from the body and at home with the Lord" (2 Corinthians 5:6-8).

The Greek of this passage is also highly revealing. The phrases "at home in the body" and "away from the Lord" in the first part of the passage are in the present tense (which, in the original Greek, indicates continuing action). Hence, we might paraphrase Paul to be saying that "while we are *continuing to be at home in the body* we are *continuing to be absent from the Lord.*"[21]

By contrast, the latter part of the passage contains two aorist infinitives: "to be away from the body" and "at home with the Lord." It is not necessary for us to pause for a Greek lesson here. I am sure that such technical details would be of little interest to most readers. All that is necessary for you to understand is that such aorists indicate a sense of "once-and-for-all." Hence, we might paraphrase it as follows: "We are of good courage, I say, and prefer rather to be once-and-for-all absent from the [flimsy, aging, and dying] mortal body and to be once-and-for-all at home with the Lord."[22]

Thus, as Bible scholar Anthony Hoekema puts it,

> Whereas the present tenses in verse 6 picture a con-
> tinuing at-homeness in the body and a continuing

away-from-homeness as to the Lord, the aorist infinitives of verse 8 point to a once-for-all momentary happening. What can this be? There is only one answer: *death*, which is an immediate transition from *being at home* in the body to *being away from home* as to the body.[23]

The moment a Christian dies, then, he or she is immediately with Christ in heaven. We are not just in the presence of the Lord, we are *intimately* present with the Lord. Note that Paul said in 2 Corinthians 5:8 that he preferred "to be away from the body and at home *with* the Lord." The Greek word for "with" in the phrase, "home *with* the Lord," suggests very close (face-to-face, as it were) fellowship. It is a word used of intimate relationships. Paul thereby indicated that the fellowship he expected to have with Christ immediately following his physical death will be one of great intimacy.

In view of such scriptural facts, it is no wonder that the world notices the joy Christians have regarding this glorious prospect of being with Christ at the moment of death. Indeed, around A.D. 125, a Greek by the name of Aristeides wrote a letter to one of his friends, trying to explain the extraordinary success of the new religion, Christianity. In his letter he said, "If any righteous man among the Christians passes from this world, they rejoice and offer thanks to God, and they accompany his body with songs and thanksgiving as if he were setting out from one place to another nearby."[24]

Serene Rest

Christians in the intermediate state enjoy a sense of serene rest in the presence of Christ. They have no tedious labors to attend to. All is tranquil. The apostle John said, "I heard a voice from heaven say, 'Write: Blessed are the dead who die in the Lord from now on.' 'Yes,' says the Spirit, 'they will rest from their labor...'" (Revelation 14:13).

This "rest" will be a *comprehensive* rest. There will be rest from all toil of the body, from all laborious work, from all the diseases and frailties of the body, from all outward sorrows, from all inward troubles, from the temptations and afflictions of Satan, and from all doubts and fears. How blessed will be that rest!

The Coming New Heavens and New Earth

While existing as a disembodied spirit in heaven in the direct presence of Christ is an awesome thing to look forward to ("better by far"—Philippians 1:23), *it gets even better after that.* After all, one day we will receive our permanent resurrection bodies (1 Corinthians 15), and God will bring about a perfect environment for our brand new bodies—*the new heavens and the new earth* (Isaiah 65:17; 66:22; 2 Peter 3:13; Revelation 21:1). Earth itself will become a part of heaven. And you and I will have the awesome privilege of living on this resurrected earth, in the heavenly city that Scripture refers to as the New Jerusalem (Revelation 21–22; more on this later).

The Intermediate State of Nonbelievers

The intermediate state of the wicked is not a pleasant topic to discuss. But inasmuch as this is a subject addressed in the Scriptures, we must at least briefly touch on it.

In a capsule, at the moment of death non-Christians go as disembodied spirits to a temporary place of suffering (Luke 16:19-31). There they await their future resurrection and judgment, with an eventual destiny in the lake of fire (Revelation 20:11-15). Following are a few details.

Experiencing Anguish

In the story Jesus told of Lazarus and the rich man, we read about what the intermediate state will be like for nonbelievers (Luke 16:19-31). You will recall that the rich man—a nonbeliever—is said to be in supreme torment. He is "in agony in this fire" (verse 24). The suffering is immeasurable.

I believe the worst torment the nonbeliever will experience, however, will be the perpetual knowledge that he or she *could have* trusted in Christ and escaped all this. The nonbeliever will always know—throughout the endless aeons and aeons of eternity—that he or she *could have* enjoyed a heavenly destiny by trusting in Christ during earthly life.

Awaiting Final Condemnation

The state of the ungodly dead in the intermediate state is described in 2 Peter 2:9: "The Lord knows how...to hold the unrighteous for the day of judgment, while continuing their punishment."

The word "hold" in this verse is a present tense, indicating that the wicked (nonbelievers) are held captive continuously. Peter is portraying them as condemned prisoners being closely guarded in a jail while awaiting future sentencing and final judgment.[25]

While God holds them there, He is said to be "continuing their punishment." The word "continuing" in this verse is also a present tense, indicating the perpetual, ongoing nature of the punishment.[26]

Punishment in the intermediate state, however, is only temporary. As noted previously, the wicked dead will eventually be resurrected (Acts 24:15) and then judged at the great white throne judgment, after which time their *eternal* punishment will begin in the lake of fire (Revelation 20:11-15).

It is sobering to realize that Scripture represents the state of unbelievers after death as a *fixed* state, and there is no second chance (Luke 16:19-31; John 8:21,24; 2 Peter 2:4,9; Jude 7,13). Once one has passed through the doorway of death, there are no further opportunities to repent and turn to Christ for salvation (Matthew 7:22-23; 10:32-33; 25:34-46). Woe unto those who reject Christ in this life.

4

ALIVE FOREVERMORE: THE FUTURE RESURRECTION

In the eternal city (the New Jerusalem), where we will live forever on the "new earth," there will be no weariness, sickness, or death. Our perfect resurrection bodies will know no limitations. Energy will never wane. Health will never be absent. There will be no further sadness nor pain. There will only be eternal vitality and joy in the presence of the Savior. Just contemplating such a future brings joy to the heart.

In the present chapter, my goal is to focus on what Scripture says about our future resurrection. Foundational to *our* resurrection, however, is the resurrection of Jesus Christ. It is here, then, that we begin.

The Resurrection of Jesus Christ

Dwight Moody, one of the great evangelists of the nineteenth century, reminded us: "You can't find directions in the New Testament on how to conduct a funeral because Jesus broke up every funeral He attended."[1] Not only did Jesus break up every funeral He attended by resurrecting the dead, He also broke up *His own* funeral by rising from the dead! (John 2:19).

Both friends and enemies of Christianity have long recognized that the resurrection of Christ is the foundation stone of the Christian faith. The apostle Paul wrote to the Corinthians: "If Christ has not been raised, your faith is futile; you are still in your sins" (1 Corinthians 15:17).

Paul realized that every doctrine of Christianity, including that of humankind's salvation, stands or falls on the doctrine of Christ's resurrection. If Christ did not rise from the dead, then Christianity is little more than an interesting museum piece. It would therefore be well worth our while to briefly examine what the Scriptures say about this incredible event.

The Evidence for Christ's Resurrection

It is utterly reasonable to believe in the resurrection of Jesus Christ inasmuch as the historical evidence overwhelmingly supports it (Matthew 28:1-15; Mark 16:1-8; Luke 24:1-12; John 20:1-18; Acts 1:3; 1 Corinthians 15:1-4; Colossians 1:18; Revelation 1:5,18):

1. The circumstances at the tomb reveal a missing body. Following His crucifixion, the body of Jesus was buried in accordance with Jewish burial customs. He was wrapped in a linen cloth, and about 100 pounds of aromatic spices—mixed together to form a gummy substance—were applied to the wrappings of cloth around His body.

After His body was placed in a solid rock tomb, an extremely large stone was rolled by means of levers against the entrance. This stone would have weighed in the neighborhood of two tons—or

4000 pounds. It is not a stone that would have been easily moved by human beings.

Roman guards were then stationed at the tomb. These strictly disciplined men were highly motivated to succeed in all they were assigned by the Roman government. Fear of cruel punishment produced flawless attention to duty, especially in the night watches. These Roman guards would have affixed on the tomb the Roman seal, a stamp representing Roman power and authority.

All this makes the situation at the tomb following Christ's resurrection highly significant. The Roman seal was broken, which meant automatic crucifixion upside-down for the person responsible. Furthermore, the large stone was moved a good distance from the entrance, as if it had been picked up and carried away. The Roman guards had also fled. The penalty in Rome for a guard leaving his position was death. We can therefore assume that they must have had a substantial reason for fleeing!

2. The biblical account has Jesus appearing first to a woman, Mary Magdalene (John 20:14-18), a fact that is a highly significant indicator of the authenticity and reliability of the resurrection account. If the resurrection story were a fabrication, made up by the disciples, no one in a first-century Jewish culture would have invented it this way. In Jewish law a woman's testimony was unacceptable in any court of law except in a very few circumstances. A fabricator would have been much more likely to portray Jesus appearing to Peter or the other male disciples first. Our biblical text, however, tells us that the Lord appeared first to Mary because, in fact, that was the way it actually happened.

Following this, Mary promptly told the disciples the glorious news. That evening, the disciples had gathered in a room with the doors shut for fear of the Jewish authorities (John 20:19). This fear was well founded, for after Jesus had been arrested, Annas the high priest specifically asked Jesus about the disciples (18:19). Jesus had also previously warned the disciples in the upper room: "If they persecuted me, they will persecute you also" (15:20). These facts no doubt lingered in their minds after Jesus was brutally crucified.

Their gloom soon turned to joy, however. The risen Christ appeared in their midst and said to them, "Peace be with you" (John 20:19). This phrase was a common Hebrew greeting (see 1 Samuel 25:6 NASB). On this occasion, however, there was added significance to Jesus' words. After their conduct on Good Friday (they all scattered like a bunch of spineless cowards after Jesus' arrest), the disciples may well have expected a rebuke from Jesus. Instead, He displayed compassion by pronouncing peace upon them.

Jesus immediately showed the disciples His hands and His side (John 20:20). The risen Lord wanted them to see that it was truly He. The wounds showed that He did not have another body but the *same* body. He was dead, but now He is alive forevermore.

3. By all accounts, the disciples came away from the crucifixion frightened and full of doubt, and yet, following Jesus' resurrection appearance to the disciples, their lives were virtually transformed. As Michael Green put it, "How have [these early followers] turned, almost overnight, into the indomitable band of enthusiasts who braved opposition, cynicism, ridicule, hardship, prison, and death on three continents, as they preached everywhere Jesus and the resurrection?"[2]

As Jews, these followers would have been predisposed to believe that no one would resurrect from the dead before the general resurrection at the end of time. It was not in their mind-set to expect a physical resurrection of Jesus. The only thing that could account for their sudden incredible transformation into powerful witnesses for Jesus was the resurrection. This is the only thing that can explain why they were even willing to die for their beliefs. Christian theologian Barry Leventhal put it this way:

When Yeshua [Jesus] died, all of his followers, in despair and fear, went into hiding. They thought that Yeshua's entire messianic movement was over. Even though they knew that the Hebrew Scriptures had prophesied that the Messiah would not see bodily corruption in the grave and that Yeshua had even predicted his own resurrection on at least three different occasions, they thought his messianic program had collapsed in utter defeat. And yet in a short time, these very same disciples appeared on the historical scene boldly proclaiming the good news of the gospel, that this Jesus who had been crucified, dead, and buried was now alive from the dead and the Lord of life and the sole determiner of men's eternal destinies.

And what did they get for such an open and bold proclamation? They endured some of the worst abuse and punishment known in their own day. In fact, many of them were tortured and even martyred for their faith in this resurrected Messiah. Men may live for a lie, but to think that thousands will die for that same lie requires a stretch of the imagination.[3]

The apostles defended their belief in Jesus and His resurrection before the Jewish Sanhedrin and the high priest, an intimidating audience to say the least. The high priest said to them: "We gave you strict orders not to teach in this name...Yet you have filled Jerusalem with your teaching and are determined to make us guilty of this man's blood" (Acts 5:28). Peter and the other apostles replied, "We must obey God rather than men! The God of our fathers raised Jesus from the dead—whom you had killed by hanging him on a tree. God exalted him to his own right hand as Prince and Savior that he might give repentance and forgiveness of sins to Israel" (Acts 5:29-31).

These witnesses seemed convinced beyond any doubt about the reality of Jesus' resurrection:

- "God has raised this Jesus to life, and we are all witnesses of the fact" (Acts 2:32).

- "You killed the author of life, but God raised him from the dead. We are witnesses of this" (Acts 3:15).

- "Then [the rulers, elders, and teachers of the law] called them in again and commanded them not to speak or teach at all in the name of Jesus. But Peter and John replied, 'Judge for yourselves whether it is right in God's sight to obey you rather than God. For we cannot help speaking about what we have seen and heard'" (Acts 4:18-20).

- "We are witnesses of everything he did in the country of the Jews and in Jerusalem. They killed him by hanging him on a tree, but God raised him from the dead on the third day and caused him to be seen" (Acts 10:39-40).

- Paul passed on the truth "that Christ died for our sins according to the Scriptures, that he was buried, that he was raised on the third day according to the Scriptures, and that he appeared to Peter, and then to the Twelve. After that, he appeared to more than five hundred of the brothers at the same time, most of whom are still living, though some have fallen asleep. Then he appeared to James, then to all the apostles, and last of all he appeared to me also, as to one abnormally born" (1 Corinthians 15:3-8).

- "Now Thomas (called Didymus), one of the Twelve,

was not with the disciples when Jesus came. So the other disciples told him, 'We have seen the Lord!' But he said to them, 'Unless I see the nail marks in his hands and put my finger where the nails were, and put my hand into his side, I will not believe it.' A week later his disciples were in the house again, and Thomas was with them. Though the doors were locked, Jesus came and stood among them and said, 'Peace be with you!' Then he said to Thomas, 'Put your finger here; see my hands. Reach out your hand and put it into my side. Stop doubting and believe.' Thomas said to him, 'My Lord and my God!' Then Jesus told him, 'Because you have seen me, you have believed; blessed are those who have not seen and yet have believed'" (John 20:24-29).

4. The many thousands of Jews who became unflinching followers of Jesus necessarily had to abandon many of their long-held sacred beliefs and practices that they formerly cherished. The only thing that can explain this radical change is the resurrection of Christ. Christian apologists Norman Geisler and Frank Turek summarize some of the beliefs and practices they gave up (an abandonment of Jewish doctrine which, according to Judaism, could lead to an eternity in hell) in order to follow Jesus:

- *The animal sacrifice system*—they replaced it forever by the one perfect sacrifice of Christ.

- *The binding supremacy of the Law of Moses*—they said it is powerless because of the sinless life of Christ.

- *Strict monotheism*—they now worshiped Jesus, the God-man, despite the fact that 1) their most cherished belief has been, "Hear, O Israel: The LORD our God, the LORD is one" (Deut. 6:4); and 2) man-worship has always been considered blasphemy and punishable by death.*

- *The Sabbath*—they no longer observed it even though they've always believed that breaking the Sabbath was punishable by death (Ex. 31:14).**

- *Belief in a conquering Messiah*—Jesus is the opposite of a conquering Messiah. He is a sacrificial lamb (at least on his first visit!).[4]

In keeping with this, Christian apologist J.P. Moreland argues that the resurrection explains

> how a large generation of Jewish people (remember, most of the early Christians were Jewish) would have been willing to risk the damnation of their own souls to hell and reject what had been sociologically embedded in their community for centuries; namely, the Law must be kept for salvation, sacrifices must be kept for salvation, the Sabbath must be kept, nontrinitarian monotheism, and there is only a political Messiah, not a dying and rising one. How does a group of people in a short time span, a society, disenfranchise themselves from that into which they had been culturally indoctrinated for centuries and risk the damnation of their

---

* "Strict monotheism" here means non-Trinitarian monotheism. Formerly, these Jews believed in one God but did not believe in the Trinity or that Jesus was God like the Father. Now, following their conversion, they still believed in monotheism (there is one God), but they also embraced the concept of the Trinity, which is the biblical teaching that there are three persons in the one God—the Father, the Son, and the Holy Spirit.

**More accurately, they no longer thought they *were required* to observe it, even though they've always believed that breaking the Sabbath was punishable by death.

own souls to hell to follow a carpenter from Nazareth? The most reasonable explanation is there was something about that man that caused this change. He was a miracle worker who rose from the dead.[5]

5. Only the resurrection of Jesus Christ could explain the conversion of hardcore skeptics in New Testament times. The apostle Paul is an example. Saul, as he was also known, delighted in breathing out "murderous threats against the Lord's disciples" (Acts 9:1). We are told that he "went to the high priest and asked him for letters to the synagogues in Damascus, so that if he found any there who belonged to the Way [that is, *Christians*], whether men or women, he might take them as prisoners to Jerusalem" (verses 1-2, insert added). Clearly, Saul was not open to following Jesus Christ, for he hated the disciples of Jesus Christ. Yet, as the rest of Acts 9 reveals, Saul had an encounter with the living, resurrected Jesus, and not only became His follower, but became the most explosive preacher and promoter of Jesus to have ever appeared on planet Earth. Only the existence of a truly resurrected and living Christ could explain such a radical conversion of a hardcore skeptic like Paul.

Another example is James, the half-brother of Jesus. James was not initially a believer in Jesus. He was a skeptic. Yet, he not only became a follower of Jesus, but became the prominent leader of the church in Jerusalem. The Jewish historian Josephus tells us that James ended up being stoned to death because of his belief in Jesus. What brought about the radical change in the heart of this skeptic? It was the resurrection of Jesus (Acts 1:14; 1 Corinthians 15:7).

Yet another example is doubting Thomas. Thomas, who had not been with the other disciples when Jesus appeared to them, refused to take the word of the other disciples about Jesus' resurrection from the dead. He said, "Unless I see the nail marks in his hands and put my finger where the nails were, and put my hand into his side, I will not believe it" (John 20:25). *Doubting* Thomas soon became *believing* Thomas, for the resurrected Lord appeared to him and invited him to touch His wounds (verses 26-27). Thomas' response to Jesus was, "My Lord and my God!" (verse 28).

6. Only the resurrection of Jesus could explain the growth and survival of the Christian church. Vast numbers of people—Jews and Gentiles—became believers in Jesus, and remained believers in Jesus, despite the fact that the Roman sword was against the throat of Christianity. Many of these people died for their testimony and commitment to Jesus. The only thing that could explain such widespread commitment is the reality of a resurrected Jesus who promised eternal life to those who followed Him.

7. There were too many appearances over too many days to too many people for the resurrection to be easily dismissed. Acts 1:3 says, "He showed himself to these men and gave many convincing proofs that he was alive. He appeared to them over a period of forty days and spoke about the kingdom of God." Moreover, "He appeared to more than five hundred of the brothers at the same time, most of whom are still living, though some have fallen asleep" (1 Corinthians 15:6). Paul mentions that many of these were "still living" because if Paul had uttered any falsehood, there were plenty of people who could have stepped forward to call Paul a liar. They did not do this, however, because the appearance of Christ was well attested.

8. The apostle Paul in 1 Corinthians 15:1-4 wrote Christ's resurrection as part of a public confession that had been handed down for years. First Corinthians was written around A.D. 55, a mere 20 years after Christ's resurrection. But biblical scholars believe the confession in 1 Corinthians 15:1-4 was formulated

within a few years of Jesus' death and resurrection. Christian theologian Gary Habermas writes: "We know that Paul wrote 1 Corinthians between A.D. 55 and 57. He indicates in 1 Corinthians 15:1-4 that he has already passed on this creed to the church at Corinth, which would mean it must predate his visit there in A.D. 51. Therefore the creed was being used within twenty years of the Resurrection, which is quite early."[6] Some scholars trace the confession back to within two years of the actual resurrection.

Weighing the Evidence

I have provided above only the briefest summary of the evidence for the resurrection of Jesus Christ. In truth, the evidence for the resurrection of Jesus Christ is both massive and formidable. It is therefore no wonder that numerous intellects have spoken with conviction about their belief in Christ's resurrection:

- Canon Westcott was a brilliant scholar at Cambridge University who concluded: "Taking all the evidence together, it is not too much to say that there is no historic incident better or more variously supported than the resurrection of Christ."[7]

- Sir Edward Clarke said, "As a lawyer, I have made a prolonged study of the evidences for the events of the first Easter Day. To me, the evidence is conclusive, and over and over again in the High Court I have secured the verdict on evidence not nearly so compelling."[8]

- Professor Thomas Arnold was the author of the famous three-volume *History of Rome* and was appointed to the Chair of Modern History at Oxford University. He was well acquainted with the value of evidence in determining historical facts. After examining all the data on Christ's resurrection, he concluded: "I know of no one fact in the history of mankind which is proved by better and fuller evidence of every sort, to the understanding of a fair inquiry, than the great sign which God has given us that Christ died and rose again from the dead."[9]

The Consensus of Church History

The resurrection of Jesus Christ from the dead has been repeatedly confirmed throughout church history. For example, the Apostles' Creed declared that the one who "suffered under Pontius Pilate, was crucified, died, and buried"—that same one "the third day rose from the dead." The Nicene Creed affirms the same, saying, "He suffered death and was buried. On the third day he rose again." The Chalcedonian Creed speaks of "following the holy Fathers" with "one consent" in affirming belief in the resurrection of Christ.

Moreover, there is a virtually unbroken testimony of the Fathers down to and through the Reformation into the modern world that Christ rose from the dead and that the resurrection was "in the flesh." For example, Irenaeus (A.D. 130–200) declared that "the Church [believes] in...the resurrection from the dead and ascension into heaven in the flesh of the beloved Christ Jesus, our Lord...." Tertullian (A.D. 160–230) concurred, saying, "He rose again the third day." Justin Martyr (second century) confirmed that Jesus did indeed "rise in the flesh." Athenagoras (second century) likewise confirmed the Resurrection. Cyril of Jerusalem (A.D. 315–386) confessed "the resurrection of the flesh." At the beginning of the Middle Ages, St. Augustine declared, "The world has come to the belief that the earthly body of Christ was received up into heaven.... [They] have believed in the resurrection of the flesh and its ascension to the heavenly places...."

This same belief in a physical resurrection of the same body that died was affirmed by the Reformers. The Lutheran Formula of Concord (A.D. 1576) affirmed that the human body of Christ was "raised from the dead." The Thirty-Nine Articles of Religion (A.D. 1562) of the Church of England affirmed that "Christ did truly rise again from the dead, and took again his body with flesh and bones." And The Westminster Confession of Faith (A.D. 1647) declared that "on the third day he arose from the dead, with the same body in which he suffered; with which he ascended into heaven...." Truly, the consensus of church history is that Christ indeed has physically risen from the dead!

Jesus Made Possible *Our* Resurrection

What is the point of all the above? It is not just to prove that Jesus is God. It is also to set the stage for the fact that Jesus' resurrection ensures *our own* resurrection from the dead.

Jesus had earlier proven that He had the divine authority to resurrect people from the dead. You may recall that following the death of Lazarus, Jesus told Lazarus's sister: "I am the resurrection and the life. He who believes in me will live, even though he dies; and whoever lives and believes in me will never die" (John 11:25-26). To prove His authority to make such statements, Jesus promptly raised Lazarus from the dead!

Jesus on another occasion affirmed, "This is the will of him who sent me, that I shall lose none of all that he has given me, but *raise them up at the last day*. For my Father's will is that everyone who looks to the Son and believes in him shall have eternal life, and I will *raise him up at the last day*" (John 6:39-40, emphasis added).

Hence, because of what Jesus Himself accomplished on our behalf, we too shall be resurrected from the dead. We can rest in the quiet assurance that even though our mortal bodies may pass away in death, turning to dust in the grave, they will be gloriously raised, never again to grow old and die. As one Bible expositor put it, "What are death, the grave, and decomposition in the presence of such power as this?... Millions that have been moldering in the dust for thousands of years shall spring up in a moment into life, immortality and eternal glory, at the voice of that blessed One."[10]

Raised Imperishable, Glorious, and Powerful

In 1 Corinthians 15:42-43, the apostle Paul said of the resurrection, "The body that is sown is perishable, it is raised imperishable; it is sown in dishonor, it is raised in glory; it is sown in weakness, it is raised in power." What a forceful statement this is of the nature of our future resurrection bodies.

Paul here graphically illustrated the contrasts between our present earthly bodies and our future resurrection bodies. The reference to sowing ("the body that is sown") is probably a metaphorical reference to burial. Just as one sows a seed in the ground, so the mortal body is "sown" in the sense that it is buried in the ground.[11] When our bodies are placed in the grave, they decompose and return to dust.

The exciting thing is what is "raised" out of the ground—the resurrection body. Paul noted that our present bodies are bodies that perish. The seeds of disease and death are ever upon them. It is a constant struggle to fight off dangerous infections. We often get sick. And all of us eventually die. It is just a question of time. Our new resurrection bodies, however, will be raised imperishable. All liability to disease and death will be forever gone. Never again will we have to worry about infections or passing away.

What did Paul mean when he said our present bodies are "sown in dishonor"? Any way you look at it, having your lifeless corpse lowered into the ground and having dirt heaped upon it is anything but a place of honor. We may try to bring honor to a funeral service by dressing our dead loved one in his or her best clothes, purchasing a fancy casket, bringing in beautiful flowers, and having people give glowing eulogies. And we *should* do all of these things. But underlying it all is the fact that death—despite our efforts to camouflage it—is something intrinsically dishonoring. After all, man was created to live forever with God, not to die and be buried in the ground.

Our new bodies, by contrast, will be utterly glorious. No dishonor here. Our new bodies will never again be subject to aging, decay, or death. Never again will our bodies be buried in the ground. How great it will be!

Paul also noted that our present bodies are characterized by weakness. From the moment we are born, the "outer man is decaying" (2 Corinthians 4:16 NASB; see also 1:8-9). Vitality decreases, illness comes, and then old age follows, with its wrinkles and decrepitude. Eventually, in old age, we may become utterly incapacitated, not able to move around and do the simplest of tasks.

By contrast, our resurrection bodies will have great power. "Our new body, like our Lord's, will be characterized by power. Sleep will not be necessary to relieve weariness or recoup spent energy. Our abilities will be enlarged and we will throw off the limitations of which we are so conscious in life on earth."[12] Never again will we tire, become weak, or become incapacitated. Words truly seem inadequate to describe the incredible differences between our present bodies (those that will be "sown" in the earth) and our future resurrection bodies. No wonder Joni Eareckson Tada, a quadriplegic, exults:

> I still can hardly believe it. I, with shriveled, bent fingers, atrophied muscles, gnarled knees, and no feeling

from the shoulders down, will one day have a new body, light, bright, and clothed in righteousness— powerful and dazzling.

Can you imagine the hope this gives someone spinal-cord injured like me? Or someone who is cerebral palsied, brain-injured, or who has multiple sclerosis? Imagine the hope this gives someone who is manic-depressive. No other religion, no other philosophy promises new bodies, hearts, and minds. Only in the Gospel of Christ do hurting people find such incredible hope.[13]

Resurrection Will Utterly Defeat Death

Resurrection is portrayed in Scripture as that which will utterly defeat death. In Hosea 13:14 God Himself declared, "I will ransom them from the power of the grave; I will redeem them from death. Where, O death, are your plagues? Where, O grave, is your destruction?"

The apostle Paul in like manner wrote,

When the perishable has been clothed with the imperishable, and the mortal with immortality, then the saying that is written will come true: "Death has been swallowed up in victory." "Where, O death, is your victory? Where, O death, is your sting?"...Thanks be to God! He gives us the victory through our Lord Jesus Christ (1 Corinthians 15:54-57).

Theologian Wayne Grudem has some wonderful words related to this passage:

The fact that our new bodies will be "imperishable" means that they will not wear out or grow old or ever be subject to any kind of sickness or disease. They will be completely healthy and strong forever. Moreover, since the gradual process of aging is part of the process by which our bodies now are subject to "corruption," it is appropriate to think that our resurrection bodies will have no sign of aging, but will have the characteristics of youthful but mature manhood or womanhood forever.[14]

Our resurrection bodies will not only be free from disease and aging, they will also be given fullness of strength and power—not infinite power like God, of course, but sufficient to do all that we desire to do in conformity with the will of God. No wonder Paul could hardly wait to be resurrected (2 Corinthians 5:1-8)!

If there were no heaven and no future resurrection from the dead, then what meaning would life have? Germany's Count Bismarck once remarked, "Without the hope of eternal life, this life is not worth the effort of getting dressed in the morning."[15] Bismarck was right. Without the hope of eternal life in heaven—without the hope of resurrection from the dead—*life is futile.*

Job knew something of the brevity and futility of life. "My days are swifter than a weaver's shuttle, and they come to an end without hope" (Job 7:6). "Man born of woman is of few days and full of trouble. He springs up like a flower and withers away; like a fleeting shadow, he does not endure" (Job 14:1-2).

Yes, this life is brief and full of sorrows. And if our existence goes no further at the grave, what is the use? This is why the apostle Paul said, "If only for this life we have hope in Christ, we are to be pitied more than all men" (1 Corinthians 15:19). But the hope that Jesus gives goes *beyond the grave,* and His resurrection guarantees that our hope is founded on fact.

Paul closed by affirming that "Christ has indeed been raised

from the dead, the firstfruits of those who have fallen asleep"
(1 Corinthians 15:20). Christ is the firstfruits. The harvest is yet to
come. All who put their trust in Him will be a part of that great
harvest of souls that will one day rise from the dead.

I can't wait!

5

THE RESURRECTION: FREQUENTLY ASKED QUESTIONS

The resurrection is a fascinating, intriguing topic. It is therefore not surprising that many people have questions regarding what our resurrection bodies will be like—especially since we'll have them for all eternity. My purpose in this chapter is to address some of the more common questions that have arisen on this topic.

Will *All* Effects of the Fall Be Gone in Our Resurrection Bodies?

Yes, absolutely. Our resurrection bodies will be perfect in every way (see 1 Corinthians 15:35-58). As Christian scholars Thomas Ice and Timothy Demy put it, "In our resurrection bodies, the effects of the Fall and of sin will be removed. The bodies will be real but without the physical limitations that we now experience and without the effects of disease, disability, or tragedy."[1] There will be no more gray hairs, no more cholesterol buildup, no more cancer or heart disease, and no more wrinkles on the face. Our bodies will no longer be susceptible to injury or disease, and there will be no allergies in heaven. Our bodies will involve absolute perfection from the top of our heads to the bottom of our feet. Death will be a thing of the past.

Will *All* Christians Experience Disembodiment in Heaven Before Being Resurrected?

No, not all. Those Christians living on earth at the time of the future Rapture will never experience disembodiment but will rather be instantly translated into their resurrection bodies. The Rapture is that glorious event in which (1) the dead in Christ will be raised from the dead, and (2) living Christians will be *instantly* translated into their resurrection bodies—and both groups will be caught up to meet Christ in the air (1 Thessalonians 4:13-17; see also 1 Corinthians 15:51-52). This event takes place prior to the future Tribulation period (see 1 Thessalonians 5:10; Revelation 3:10). All other Christians (that is, all those *not* alive on earth at the time of the Rapture) will experience disembodiment in heaven for a time prior to their eventual resurrection.

Why Is Our Present Body Compared to a "Tent" in Scripture?

We briefly touched on this issue in the previous chapter. The apostle Paul compared our present earthly bodies to *tents* and our permanent resurrection bodies to *buildings* (2 Corinthians 5:1-4). Paul was speaking in terms that his listeners would have readily understood. After all, the temporary tabernacle of Israel's wanderings in the wilderness (essentially, a giant tentlike structure) was eventually replaced with a permanent building (temple) when Israel entered the Promised Land. In like manner, the temporary "tent" (or body) in which believers now dwell will be replaced one day with an eternal, immortal, imperishable body (see 1 Corinthians 15:42,53-54).

One commentator paraphrased Paul's words this way: "Don't take your physical situation too seriously. Your body is fine to camp out in for a while, but before long, the tent will begin to sag; a stake or two will be lost along the way; seams will begin to tear." He then gets to the heart of the issue when he says: "Our Father is so good to gently remind us every time we look in the mirror that we're rushing toward eternity. Paul was one who truly understood that his body was only a temporary dwelling."[2]

Particularly relevant is Paul's statement in 2 Corinthians 5:4: "For while we are in this tent [of our present mortal body], we groan and are burdened, because we do not wish to be unclothed [without a body] but to be clothed with our heavenly dwelling [resurrection body], so that what is mortal [our earthly body] may be swallowed up by life [resurrection]" (inserts added for clarification). Paul here indicates that being "unclothed"—that is, being without a physical body as a result of death—is a state of incompletion, and for him carries a sense of "nakedness." Even though departing to be with Christ in a disembodied state is "better by far" than life on earth (Philippians 1:23; see also verse 21), Paul's true yearning was to be "clothed" with a physically resurrected body (see 2 Corinthians 5:6-8).[3] And that yearning will be fully satisfied on that future day of resurrection at the Rapture.

Meanwhile, like Paul said, "we groan" (2 Corinthians 5:4). *Why so?* Because our bodies are burdened by sin, sickness, sorrow, and death. Commentator Albert Barnes explains it this way: "The sense is…that the body is subjected to so many pains, and to so much suffering, as to make us earnestly desire to be invested with that body which shall be free from all susceptibility to suffering."[4] Or, more to the point, "We groan because our 'tents' are showing signs of use, because our bodies are wearing out."[5]

How Is the Holy Spirit a "Deposit" of What Is to Come?

The apostle Paul, in 2 Corinthians 5:5, affirmed that God has given us the Holy Spirit as a deposit of what is to come in the afterlife. Contextually, Paul had just referred to our earthly bodies as *tents* and our future resurrection bodies as *buildings* (2 Corinthians 5:1-3). While still existing in our mortal bodies, however, Paul says we groan, as noted above (see verse 4). Moreover, Paul said, we ideally prefer to *immediately* receive resurrection bodies instead of temporarily becoming disembodied spirits. This is so, despite the fact that being a disembodied spirit with Christ in heaven is "better by far" than our present lives on earth (Philippians 1:23).

It is in this specific context that Paul said that God has given us the Holy Spirit as a "deposit" of what is yet to come. The word "deposit" was used among the Greeks to refer to a pledge that guaranteed final possession of an item. It was sometimes used of an engagement ring which acted as a guarantee that the marriage would take place. The Holy Spirit is a "deposit" in the sense that His presence in our lives guarantees our eventual total transformation and glorification into the likeness of Christ's glorified resurrection body (see Philippians 3:21). The Holy Spirit in us is virtually a guarantee of what is to come.

This helps us to maintain an eternal perspective. It is true that our present bodies are wearing down. They've been infected by a fatal disease known as sin. One day, they will simply cease functioning (they will fall down like a flimsy tent). By contrast, our resurrection bodies in heaven will never again wear down, never again get sick, and never again die (they will be as solid and sturdy as a building). Pastor Paul Powell tells us that "there will be no blind eyes in heaven. No withered arms or legs in heaven. No pain or agony there. Tears will be gone. Death will be gone. Separation will be gone. This will be the ultimate healing. Then and only then, we will be free at last."[6] Keeping this truth before our minds can really put "wind in our sails" when we seem to be stagnating on the sea of suffering.

Will Our Resurrection Bodies Be *Physical* Bodies?

Absolutely yes! To make my case, I need to first establish that Jesus' resurrection body was a physical resurrection body. Here's what you need to know:

1. The tomb was empty. All four Gospels (Matthew 28; Mark 16; Luke 24; John 20) report that the tomb in which Jesus was buried and which the Romans guarded was empty three days later.

2. Jesus' resurrection body retained the crucifixion scars. Over a 40-day period, Christ—in the same body that had been crucified and buried—appeared to over 500 people on 12 different occasions, showing on 2 of these occasions the very scars from His crucifixion (Luke 24:39; John 20:27). In one appearance Jesus connected His own self-identity with this body, saying, "Look at my hands and my feet. It is I myself! Touch me and see; a ghost does not have flesh and bones, as you see I have" (Luke 24:39). So, either it was the same body in which He was crucified or else Jesus was being dishonest!

3. Jesus' resurrection body had "flesh and bones." As noted above, the body was not a "spirit" but rather had "flesh and bones" (Luke 24:39). This reveals that it was the *same* body of "flesh" in which Jesus was incarnated (John 1:14) and later raised (Acts 2:31), and in which He continually lived and continues to live today (see 1 John 4:2; 2 John 7). Indeed, in these latter two texts, John indicates that denials of this are rooted in the spirit of the Antichrist.

4. Jesus ate food in His resurrection body. In fact, Jesus ate physical food four times after the resurrection (Luke 24:30; 24:42-43; John 21:12-13; Acts 1:4) and offered it as proof that He had a real physical body.

5. Jesus' resurrection body was touched by others. Scripture indicates that on two occasions Jesus' body was actually touched (Matthew 28:9; John 20:27-28) and on another occasion He offered His body to be touched (Luke 24:39-40). When doubting Thomas was challenged by Jesus to touch Him, he worshipfully cried out: "My Lord and my God" (John 20:28).

6. Jesus' resurrection body was visible to the naked eye. It was both seen with the naked eye (Matthew 28:17) and heard with natural ears (John 20:15-16). The same words are used in the New Testament to describe seeing and hearing Jesus in His pre-resurrection body. The witnesses who beheld the resurrected Jesus did not have spiritual visions but rather made literal observations with the natural senses.

Some may respond by asking why the disciples did not recognize Jesus on occasion. Scripture provides the answers. Once, "they were kept from recognizing him" (Luke 24:16) and were perplexed (Luke 24:17-21). Some were in sorrow (John 20:11-15). Once it was still dark (John 20:1,14-15). On another occasion the distance was great (John 21:4). Those behind a closed door were startled when He suddenly appeared (Luke 24:36-37). Some were disbelieving (John 20:24-25). Others were spiritually dull (Luke 24:25-26). But the fact is that these were only initial and temporary responses. Before the appearance was over in each case, they were so totally convinced of His identity that they were willing to die for Him, and within weeks were turning the world upside down in His behalf (fulfilling the Great Commission).

7. The word "body" (Greek: soma), used to describe the resurrection body in 1 Corinthians 15:44, always means a physical body in the New Testament when used of individual human beings. Further, using an analogy from planting a seed, the body that is "sown" in death is the *same* body that is raised (1 Corinthians 15:35-44). What is more, the resurrection is *from among* (Greek: *ek*) the dead. This means Jesus' body was raised from the graveyard (Luke 24:46) where physical corpses are buried (see also Acts 13:29-30).

Having thoroughly established the physicality of Jesus' resurrection body, the point I now wish to emphasize is that *our* resurrection bodies will be just like Jesus' resurrection body in this regard. The apostle Paul said that Christ "will transform our lowly bodies so that *they will be like his glorious body*" (Philippians 3:21, emphasis added). John likewise said, "Dear friends, now we are children of God, and what we will be has not yet been made known. But we know that when he appears, *we shall be like him*, for we shall see him as he is" (1 John 3:2, emphasis added). So, we will not be ethereal spirits floating around in space for all eternity. Rather, we will be *physically* resurrected and we will live in a *physical* place (see John 14:1-3).

Some have objected and asked how our resurrection bodies can be physical if the Bible says that "flesh and blood" cannot inherit the kingdom of God. In 1 Corinthians 15:50 we read the apostle Paul's words: "I declare to you, brothers, that flesh and blood cannot inherit the kingdom of God..." It is crucial to recognize that the term "flesh and blood" is simply a Jewish idiom used in Scripture to refer to *mortal, perishable humanity.* This verse is saying that mortal human beings in their present perishable bodies cannot inherit heaven. Mortal humanity must be made immortal humanity in order to survive in heaven. The resurrection body will be endowed with special qualities that will enable it to adapt perfectly to life in God's presence. As 1 Corinthians 15:53 puts it, "The perishable must clothe itself with the imperishable, and the mortal with immortality." So, the resurrection body will be physical, immortal, and imperishable.

Will Resurrection Pose a Problem for Those Who Have Been Cremated, or Blown Up in a War?

I am sometimes asked about people who have been cremated, or perhaps blown up in a war, or maybe eaten by wild animals, or maybe eaten by sharks in the ocean. Will it be any problem for God to physically resurrect such people from the dead? No, not in the slightest degree. As noted previously, 2 Corinthians 5:1 promises: "Now we know that if the earthly tent we live in is destroyed, we have a building from God, an eternal house in heaven, not built by human hands." It does not matter *how* our "earthly tent" (body) is destroyed; all that matters is that God, with His matchless power, will raise it from the dead. Keep in mind that even those who are buried eventually dissolve into dust and bones. So, regardless of whether we are buried or cremated (or blown up or eaten by animals or sharks), we can all look forward to a permanent resurrection body that will never be subject to death and decay. As Reformer John Calvin put it so well, "Since God has all the elements at his disposal, no difficulty can prevent him from commanding the earth, the fire, and the water to give up what they seem to have destroyed."[7] God, the Creator of the entire universe (Genesis 1; John 1:3; Colossians 1:16; Hebrews 1:2; Revelation 4:11), will experience no difficulty in resurrecting our bodies from the dead (Job 19:25-27; Psalm 49:15; Isaiah 26:19; John 6:39-40,44,54; 1 Corinthians 6:14; 1 Thessalonians 4:13-17; Revelation 20:4-6).

What Age Will Our Resurrection Bodies Appear?

I am often asked, "Will our resurrection bodies look just like they looked at the moment of death? Will babies who died in infancy be resurrected to appear as babies? Will old men be resurrected to appear as old men, even though they are now full of resurrected vitality and youth? Will people with missing limbs still have missing limbs in their resurrection bodies?"

I personally believe that we will all be resurrected at an ideal, youthful age—perhaps in the thirties. After all, God created Adam and Eve with apparent age (some Bible expositors guesstimate the thirties), and perhaps the age that God created them may be considered an optimal stage of physical development since God declared His creation "very good" (Genesis 1:31). Likewise, as the great Thomas Aquinas (1225–1274) recognized, when Jesus died, He was in His thirties, and was resurrected in the same thirtysomething body.[8] So, maybe all of us will be resurrected to appear in our thirties, but all of us—whether we die in infancy or old age—will be recognizable by all others (see 1 Thessalonians 4:13-17).

In keeping with this, theologian Norman Geisler suggests that babies will be matured in heaven: "Heaven is a place of maturity and perfection, and babies stunted in their growth, short of maturity, would not reflect a state of perfection. It seems to better befit God's nature and plan for those who were not granted earthly maturity to attain it in heaven."[9] Moreover, it seems to befit God's nature and plan for missing limbs to be fully restored in the resurrection body, for anything less would not be perfect.

Will We Wear Clothes?

Sometimes people ask, "Will we be wearing clothes in heaven?" After all, when God first created Adam and Eve, He created them naked (Genesis 2:25), and it wasn't until after they sinned that they first felt shame and started wearing clothes (3:7). So, some wonder whether we will wear clothes in our sinless state in heaven?

Personally, I think so—and I base my opinion largely on the Book of Revelation. Revelation 1:13, speaking of the glorified Christ, tells us that He was "dressed in a robe reaching down to his feet and with a golden sash round his chest." Revelation 3:5, speaking of members of the church in Sardis, tells us that "he who overcomes will...be dressed in white." Revelation 7:9 speaks of a multitude of redeemed people in heaven who are "wearing white robes" and "holding palm branches in their hands." Revelation 19:8, speaking of the church as the bride of Christ, tells us that "fine linen, bright and clean, was given her to wear." When Christ leaves heaven and comes again at the second coming, He will return "dressed in a robe dipped in blood" (Revelation 19:13). Verses such as these lead me to believe that all of us will be dressed in the afterlife.

Can We Eat Food in Heaven?

Some Christians have claimed that we will not eat food in heaven because Romans 14:17 states that "the kingdom of God is not a matter of eating and drinking, but of righteousness, peace and joy in the Holy Spirit." However, in context, this verse has nothing to do with the afterlife or heaven. Contextually, Paul was simply teaching that we should be cautious not to cause other Christians to stumble by what we eat and drink while we are on earth.

I previously mentioned that Jesus ate physical food four times after His resurrection from the dead (Luke 24:30; 24:42-43; John 21:12-13; Acts 1:4). Our resurrection bodies will be like Jesus' resurrection body (see Philippians 3:21; 1 John 3:2). This would seem to indicate that we too will be able to eat food in our resurrection bodies. However, as one theologian noted, we will eat "for enjoyment, not for sustenance—for pleasure rather than necessity."[10]

That our resurrection bodies will be able to consume food is confirmed in Revelation 22:1-2, where we read of the heavenly city (the New Jerusalem): "Then the angel showed me the river of the water of life, as clear as crystal, flowing from the throne of God and of the Lamb down the middle of the great street of the city. On each side of the river stood the tree of life, bearing twelve crops of fruit, yielding its fruit every month. And the leaves of the tree are for the healing of the nations." Bible expositor John MacArthur makes the following observation:[11]

> The Greek word translated "healing" is *therapeia,* from which we get the English word therapeutic. John is saying that the leaves of the tree of life somehow enrich the heavenly life—if only through the pure joy of eating. The water of life is also there for the sheer pleasure of drinking. No food will be needed in heaven, but incredible gourmet delights will nonetheless be enjoyed. Again this underscores the truth that God's design for us is that we may enjoy Him forever. Much of heaven is designed for sheer pleasure—both the pleasure of God and the pleasure of His people.[11]

While I personally agree with MacArthur that eating food will not actually be needed for us to survive in heaven, there are some Christians who believe that eating the fruit of the Tree of Life will be a necessity. Those who hold to this view suggest that "the fruit of the tree of life is what will give us immortality, just as it did for Adam and Eve originally."[12] In fairness, there is no verse in the New Testament that explicitly states this.

Randy Alcorn suggests that we may be vegetarians in the afterlife. After all, animal death did not occur until after humankind's fall and the subsequent curse (Genesis 3). Since there will be no fallenness and no curse in heaven, it may be that animals will no longer be eaten.[13]

Whether or not this is so, one thing is for certain: We will never get fat if we eat in heaven! So, there is no need to ever worry about having to go on a diet in heaven. *Awesome!*

Will We Have Heightened Senses in Our Resurrection Bodies?

Is it possible that in our future resurrection bodies, we will have heightened senses of sight, hearing, smell, taste, and touch? It seems a good possibility. As an example, I believe that even though human beings on earth are not normally able to perceive angels (since they are invisible spirit creatures—Hebrews 1:14), we will be able to perceive them in heaven just as easily as they perceive us (this may be implied in 1 Corinthians 6:3; see also Revelation 5:11-14). Our ability to perceive will apparently be much heightened.

Interestingly, Randy Alcorn suggests the possibility that our eyes might have the capability of functioning as a microscope and a telescope—thereby enabling us to behold all the wonders of God's glorious new heavens and new earth. He also suggests that our eyes might be able to behold far more colors than at present. Perhaps, also, our senses of hearing and smelling might be greatly sharpened. If even our present bodies are "fearfully and wonderfully made," then this must be much more so of our future resurrection bodies.[14]

Will Our Resurrection Bodies Be Able to Exist in God's Direct Glorious Presence?

Yes, I believe so! One of the most exciting and meaningful things to me personally regarding the resurrection body is that it will be a body specially suited for dwelling in the unveiled presence of God in all of His glory.

Scripture informs us that God dwells in "unapproachable

light" (1 Timothy 6:16; see also Psalm 104:2). So brilliant and glorious is this light that no mortal can survive in its midst.

There are occasions in Scripture in which a believer catches a brief glimpse of God's glory, and the result is always the same. The believer falls to his knees as if he is about to die. As one Bible expositor put it, "Such an unveiled view of God is impossible for mortal men."[15]

The apostle John, for example, saw Christ in His glory and "fell at his feet as though dead" (Revelation 1:17). When Abraham beheld the Almighty, he "fell facedown" (Genesis 17:3). When Manoah and his wife saw a manifestation of the Lord, they "fell with their faces to the ground" (Judges 13:20). Ezekiel, upon seeing the glory of God, "fell facedown" (Ezekiel 3:23; 43:3; 44:4).

We often read about the "glory" of God and Christ in the Scriptures. The word "glory," when used of God, refers to the luminous manifestation of God.[16] This definition is borne out by the many ways the word is used in Scripture. For example, brilliant light consistently accompanies the divine manifestation of His glory (Matthew 17:2-3; 1 Timothy 6:16; Revelation 1:16). Moreover, the word *glory* is often linked with verbs of seeing (Exodus 16:7; 33:18; Isaiah 40:5) and verbs of appearing (Exodus 16:10; Deuteronomy 5:24), both of which emphasize the visible nature of God's glory.

In our finite mortality, we simply cannot exist in the unveiled presence of God. Because God lives in unapproachable light, our bodies—as presently constituted—cannot exist in His presence. But all this will one day change. When we receive our glorified resurrection bodies, they will be specially suited to dwelling in the presence of God. Just as the caterpillar has to be changed into the butterfly in order to inherit the air, so we have to be changed in order to inherit heaven. And once we are changed, we will be able to fellowship with Him face-to-face (see Revelation 21:1-3).[17]

Truly, the day that our perishable mortal bodies are resurrected into imperishable, glorious bodies is a day to yearn for. For "the trumpet will sound, the dead will be raised imperishable, and we will be changed. For the perishable must clothe itself with the imperishable, and the mortal with immortality. When the perishable has been clothed with the imperishable, and the mortal with immortality, then the saying that is written will come true: 'Death has been swallowed up in victory'" (1 Corinthians 15:52-54). What a glorious day that will be!

6

HEAVEN: FREQUENTLY ASKED QUESTIONS

Heaven is a fascinating subject. Whenever I've been blessed to lead a discussion on this topic, I've inevitably encountered all kinds of interesting questions. My goal in this chapter is to biblically answer the most common among them.

What Are the Three "Heavens" of Scripture?

Words can carry different meanings in different contexts. For example, the English word "trunk" can refer to the front of an elephant, the back of a car, the bottom of a tree, the rear end of a man, or a suitcase, all depending on the context. Biblical words are the same way.

I point this out because the Scriptures make reference to the "third heaven"—which, according to context, is the ineffable and glorious dwelling place of God in all His glory (2 Corinthians

12:2; see also Deuteronomy 26:15; Psalm 14:2; Matthew 6:9-10; 18:10; 28:2). It is elsewhere called the "highest heaven" (1 Kings 8:27,30; 2 Chronicles 2:6).

If God's abode is the "third" heaven, then what are the first and second heavens? Scripture gives us the answer. The first heaven is that of the earth's atmosphere (Genesis 1:20,26,28; 8:2; Deuteronomy 28:12; Job 35:5; Psalm 147:8; Matthew 8:20; 13:32; 16:2-3). The second heaven is that of the stellar universe (Genesis 1:14-15,17; 15:5; Deuteronomy 4:19; 17:3; 28:62; Acts 2:19-20; Hebrews 11:12).

Why Will There Be *New* Heavens and a *New* Earth?

Scripture indicates that God will one day create *new* heavens and a *new* earth (Revelation 21:1). Many have thus wondered, Which heaven (or heavens) will pass away and be made new?

The only heavens that have been negatively affected by human-kind's fall are the first and second heavens—earth's atmosphere and the stellar universe, part of "all creation" (Romans 8:20-22), including the earth itself (Genesis 3:17; 5:29). The entire physical universe is running down and decaying. But the third heaven— God's perfect and glorious dwelling place—remains untouched by human sin. It needs no renewal. This heaven subsists in moral and physical perfection, and undergoes no change.[1]

Hence, when Scripture makes reference to the passing away of the old heaven and earth, and speaks of a new heaven and earth (Isaiah 65:17; 66:22; 2 Peter 3:13; Revelation 21:1), the "heaven" referred to is not God's dwelling place but rather the first and second heavens. When these heavens along with the earth are made new, there will be a much wider meaning for the third heaven. As Bible scholar Merrill Unger has put it, the term "heaven" "will embrace the new heaven, the new earth, the New Jerusalem, and indeed a sinless universe...In fact, in the eternal state, the term "heaven" will comprehend the entire universe, exclusive of the one isolation ward for all sinners, called, Gehenna, or the lake of fire."[2]

Why Is Heaven Called a "Country"?

Hebrews 11 is the Faith Hall of Fame in the Bible. In this pivotal chapter we read of the eternal perspective of many of the great faith warriors in biblical times. Here the word "country" is used as a metaphor pointing to the wonderful destiny of heaven for the biblical saints:

> All these people were still living by faith when they died. They did not receive the things promised; they only saw them and welcomed them from a distance. And they admitted that they were aliens and strangers on earth. People who say such things show that they are looking for a *country of their own.* If they had been thinking of the country they had left, they would have had opportunity to return. Instead, they were longing for a *better country—a heavenly one* (Hebrews 11:13- 16, emphasis added).

This passage tells us that the great warriors of the faith in biblical times were not satisfied with earthly, temporal things—things that are passing away. Instead, they looked forward to "a better country." And what a glorious "country" it is. Eighteenth-century Bible expositor John Gill contemplated how

> the heavenly country is full of light and glory; having the delightful breezes of divine love, and the comfortable gales of the blessed Spirit; here is no heat of persecution, nor coldness, nor chills of affection; here is plenty of most delicious fruits, no hunger nor thirst; and here are riches, which are solid, satisfying,

durable, safe and sure: many are the liberties and privileges here enjoyed; here is a freedom from a body subject to diseases and death, from a body of sin and death, from Satan's temptations, from all doubts, fears, and unbelief, and from all sorrows and afflictions.[3]

Christians of all ages, like the Old Testament personalities mentioned in the Faith Hall of Fame, have looked forward with great anticipation to the heavenly country. Presently we are but pilgrims in another land, making our way to the heavenly country. Take comfort in this realization!

Is Heaven a Physical Place?

Many throughout church history have thought of heaven as a kind of ethereal, spiritual dimension. The biblical evidence, however, indicates that heaven will be a physical place, something seemingly required by the fact that you and I will be physically resurrected from the dead (1 Corinthians 15:35-53), just as Jesus was. (Recall that the resurrected Jesus said to the disciples: "Look at my hands and my feet. It is I myself! Touch me and see; a ghost does not have flesh and bones, as you see I have"—Luke 24:39.)

In fact, Scripture indicates that the new heavens and new earth will be physical in nature, and we will physically dwell in the new heavens and new earth for all eternity. Theologian Wayne Grudem suggests that "the fact that we will have resurrection bodies like Christ's resurrection body indicates that heaven will be a place, for in such physical bodies (made perfect, never to become weak or die again), we will inhabit a specific place at a specific time, just as Jesus now does in his resurrection body."[4] Christian scholars Kenneth Boa and Robert Bowman likewise affirm that "the hope of God's people is not an ethereal heaven but a new universe in which redeemed human beings will live."[5] Scholar Anthony Hoekema agrees, noting that "resurrected bodies are not intended just to float in space.... They call for a new earth on which to live and to work, glorifying God. The doctrine of the resurrection of the body, in fact, makes no sense whatever apart from the doctrine of the new earth."[6]

There are numerous indications in the New Testament that heaven will be a physical place. For example, as noted previously in this book, Jesus in John 14:1-3 affirmed; "In my Father's *house* are many *rooms;* if it were not so, I would have told you. I am going there to prepare *a place* for you. And if I go and prepare *a place* for you, I will come back and take you to be with me that you also may be where I am" (emphasis added). The words "house," "rooms," and "a place" suggest a physical place where the physically resurrected redeemed will forever live.

In Revelation 21:9–22:5, heaven is likewise described in terms that indicate a physical place, for the heavenly city has walls, gates, foundations, a street, river, trees, and more. While the Book of Revelation contains a great deal of symbolism, there is no indication in the context that heaven is intended to be understood as anything other than a physical place.

Where Is Heaven Located?

As one might expect, Christians have expressed different viewpoints regarding where heaven might be located. On the one hand, some Christians suggest that heaven is somewhere in our space-time universe—far, far away, perhaps shrouded by a cloud of God's glory. Some believe that perhaps heaven is located in the north of our universe, citing words about God found in Job 37:22: "*Out of the north* he comes in golden splendor; God comes in awesome majesty" (emphasis added; see also 26:7). A supportive evidence for this view is that at the ascension, Jesus literally went up into the sky as witnessed by some of His disciples—that is, He "was taken up before their very eyes, and a cloud hid him from their sight" (Acts 1:9). This same text indicates that one day, at the second coming, Christ will return to the same place (the Mount of Olives) from which He left (Acts 1:10-11; see Zechariah 14:4).[7]

Other Christians suggest that perhaps heaven is located in an entirely different dimension than ours. In favor of this view is that there are several occasions when Jesus seemed to enter and depart from the space-time dimension when in His resurrection body. For example, after Jesus made a resurrection appearance to some of His followers, He "disappeared from their sight" (Luke 24:31). Moreover, Scripture tells us when some of His disciples were in a house, "Though the doors were locked, Jesus came and stood among them and said, 'Peace be with you'" (John 20:26). Some claim He appeared from another dimension. Further, Mark 1:10, a verse which speaks of Jesus' baptism, says, "As Jesus was coming up out of the water, he saw heaven being *torn open* and the Spirit descending on him like a dove" (emphasis added). Some thus claim that heaven must exist in a different dimension. Supporting this view is the modern scientific paradigm which suggests that there are multiple dimensions in the universe.[8]

How Long Will Heaven Exist?

Heaven will last forever. Some theologians suggest that heaven will last as long as God exists, and since God will last forever, then heaven will last forever. It is also suggested that since heaven is the place where the redeemed of all ages will experience eternal life, then heaven itself must be just as eternal as eternal life. Titus 1:2 speaks of "the hope of eternal life, which God, who does not lie, promised before the beginning of time." Jesus Himself promised that the righteous will go "to eternal life" (Matthew 25:46). Moreover, in the Book of Revelation, John declared: "I heard every creature in heaven and on earth and under the earth and on the sea, and all that is in them, singing: 'To him who sits on the throne and to the Lamb be praise and honor and glory and power, *for ever and ever!*' " (Revelation 5:13).[9] We might also surmise that since the Architect and Builder of the New Jerusalem (the eternal city) is none other than Christ Himself (see John 14:1-3), then the city will be absolutely perfect in every way, and will not be subject to decay or deterioration. In other words, it will last forever.

Is There Time in Heaven?

If heaven is a physical place, as we have argued, then is there time in heaven as well? Many Christians believe there are indications in Scripture that there will indeed be time—a "succession of moments"—in our heavenly existence. In favor of this view is the fact that the Book of Revelation indicates that we will sing in heaven (see Revelation 5:9; 14:3; 15:3). How can there be songs with a beat, with lyrics that are sung, with singers transitioning from verse to chorus, with a beginning and an end, without there being time? It seems unimaginable.

Further, in Revelation 6:9-10 some Christians who will be martyred in the future Tribulation period ask God, "How long, Sovereign Lord, holy and true, until you judge the inhabitants of the earth and avenge our blood?" The phrase "how long" indicates a sense of time passing in heaven.

Moreover, God's people are said to "serve him day and night in his temple" (Revelation 7:15). The opening of the seven seals (related to the seven seal judgments) are sequential (with intervals in between), and reference is made to "silence in heaven for about half an hour" after the opening of the seventh seal (Revelation 8:1). In Revelation 22:2 we read that the Tree of Life yields its fruit "every month."

Still further, if those who reside in heaven rejoice *whenever* a sinner repents on temporal earth (Luke 15:7), this would seem to indicate a sense of "moments passing" in heaven, since not everyone repents at the same time, but rather do so at different times, as time passes by, year in and year out, from the first century to the present.

Of course, God Himself is a timeless being. He is not bound by viewing events as a "succession of moments." Because God transcends time—because He is above time—He can see the past, present, and future as a single intuitive act. God's limitless knowledge of all things is from the vantage point of eternity, so that the past, present, and future are all encompassed in one ever-present "now" to Him.[10] The entire panoramic sweep of all human history—past, present, and future—lies before the all-seeing eye of God. However, simply because God is *beyond* time does not mean that He cannot act *within* time. From a biblical perspective, God is *eternal,* but He can do *temporal* things. God's acts take place *within time,* but His attributes remain *beyond time.*[11]

I should also note that there are some philosophically minded Christians who are careful to stipulate that the actual *nature* of redeemed human beings in heaven will be timeless, but they will still have the capacity to engage in *acts* that involve time. The reasoning goes like this (brace yourself for very deep thoughts):

> Because time is a measurement *of change* according to a *before* and an *after,* we cannot be temporal in heaven; if we were temporal, then we would *still be changing;* however, we will be perfect, and what is perfect *does not need to change....* [Therefore] our state...will be one like that of the angels, who are not in time *by nature* but can be related to it *by activity.*[12]

If that just flew right over your head, don't worry about it. The bottom line is that you and I will be perfect in every way in heaven, and we will be aware of—and able to participate in—events that involve the passing of time.

Do Human Beings Become Angels When They Go to Heaven?

Today there continues to be a widespread idea that human beings become angels at the moment of death. Even while doing research for this book, I read in a newspaper of a widely beloved woman who died, and one of the mourners at the funeral service commented: "Although we on earth have lost a great lady, heaven has gained a glorious angel."[13] This view is all too common.

There is no scriptural justification for such an idea. Scripture tells us that Christ created "all things...in heaven and...on earth" (Colossians 1:16), which would include angels. We see the distinction between humans and angels reflected in a number of biblical passages. For example, Psalm 8:5 indicates that man was made lower than the "heavenly beings" (angels) but shall be made higher than the angels in the afterlife (in heaven). In Hebrews 12:22-23 the "myriads of angels" are clearly distinguished from the "spirits of righteous made perfect" (NASB). First Corinthians 6:3 tells us that there is a time coming when believers (in the afterlife) will judge over the angels. Moreover, 1 Corinthians 13:1 draws a distinction between the languages of human beings and those of angels. Clearly, human beings and angels are portrayed as different classes of beings in the Bible. So, when a loved one dies, it is incorrect to conclude that they've now become an angel in heaven.

Some have wondered *when* the angels were created. Many theologians believe the angels were created sometime prior to the creation of the earth—and I think there is good evidence to support this view. Job 38:7, for example, makes reference to the "sons of God" (NASB) singing at the time the earth was created.

Theologians believe these "sons of God" in Job 38 are angels. After all, the term "sons of God" is used elsewhere in Job in reference to angels (see Job 1:6; 2:1). If Job 38:7 is to be taken as referring to angels, as there is every reason for it to be, then even before the creation of the material universe (and human beings) there was a vast world of spirit beings. These angelic spirit beings sang as a massive choir when God created the earth. What a moment that must have been!

Who Are the Occupants of Heaven?

Who specifically dwells in heaven? The short answer is God, angels, and Christians. Let's take a look at the details:

God Dwells in Heaven

First and foremost, heaven is where God Himself dwells. Heaven is God's natural habitat. We read in Psalm 102:19 that the Lord looks down "from his sanctuary on high," and "from heaven" He views the earth. We are told, "The LORD has established his throne in heaven, and his kingdom rules over all" (Psalm 103:19). The Lord says, "Heaven is my throne, and the earth is my footstool..." (Acts 7:49).

Some have wondered how this relates to the fact that God is omnipresent (or everywhere-present). How can an omnipresent being dwell in one place? Solomon even affirmed: "The heavens, even the highest heaven, cannot contain you. How much less this temple I have built" (1 Kings 8:27).

J. Sidlow Baxter suggests that "God is everywhere immanent throughout the universe, while yet there is one place, inconceivable as it is to our finite minds, where apparently his throne and presence are ineffably concentrated."[14] John MacArthur agrees, noting that when we say that God *dwells* in heaven, we are not saying that He is *contained* in heaven. And yet heaven is His unique home, where His sovereign throne is, the heart and center of His providential operations throughout the universe, and the place where He is most perfectly worshiped by His creatures.[15] It is in this limited sense that we say that God "dwells" in heaven.

We can also biblically affirm that Jesus—the second person of our omnipresent Trinitarian God—dwells in heaven. Scripture indicates that Jesus came *from* heaven and was born as a human being, grew up, completed His three-year ministry, died on the cross to secure salvation for those who would believe, resurrected from the dead, and then ascended *back into* heaven. As Christ ascended into heaven, it may well be that thousands of angels accompanied Him while en route. Some scholars believe a hint of this may be found in Psalm 68:17-18, which makes reference to when the Lord "ascended on high" accompanied by "tens of thousands and thousands of thousands" of angels.

What an awesome moment it must have been when Christ, clothed in a glorified human body, re-entered heaven, His natural habitat. What shouts of glory must have then been heard among the cherubim, the seraphim, the dominions, thrones, powers, and angelic authorities of heaven! A mighty hallelujah chorus no doubt swept through the heavens as He seated Himself "in the heavenly realms, far above all rule and authority, power and dominion, and every title that can be given, not only in the present age, but also in the one to come" (Ephesians 1:20-21).[16]

As He now is in heaven, Jesus is awesome to contemplate. The Book of Revelation speaks in dazzling terms of the ascended Christ. I can do no better than to quote Isbon T. Beckwith, who, in his commentary on Revelation, has summarized:

> Nowhere else are found these wonderful scenes revealing to the eye and ear the majesty of Christ's ascended state, and these numerous utterances

expressing in terms applicable to God alone the truth of His divine nature and power. He is seen...having the semblance of a man, yet glorified with attributes by which the Old Testament writers have sought to portray the glory of God; His hair is white as snow, His face shines with the dazzling light of the sun, His eyes are a flame of fire, His voice as the thunder of many waters; He announces Himself as eternal, as the one who though He died is the essentially living One, having all power over death (1:13-18). He appears in the court of heaven as coequal with God in the adoration offered by the highest hosts of heaven and by all the world (5:6-14).... He is the Alpha and Omega, the first and the last, the beginning and the end (22:13; 1:17; 2:8) a designation which God also utters of Himself (1:8, cf. Isa. 44:6; 48:12); worship is offered to Him in common with God (7:10; 5:13) a worship which angelic beings are forbidden to receive (19:10); doxologies are raised to Him as to God (1:6); the throne of God is His throne, the priests of God are His priests (3:21; 22:1; 20:6); life belongs essentially to Him as to God (1:18; 4:9,10).[17]

The Angels Dwell in Heaven

Though angels apparently have access to the entire universe, it would seem to be the testimony of Scripture that angels actually live in heaven but are sent on specific errands or assignments outside of heaven (see Daniel 9:21-23; see also Mark 13:32).[18] There are numerous passages in Scripture that speak of heaven as the primary habitat of angels. For example:

- Second Chronicles 18:18 discusses "the LORD sitting on his throne with all the host of heaven standing on his right and on his left." The "host of heaven" has specific reference to the angelic realm.

• Daniel 7:10 makes reference to "thousands upon thousands" of attendants (presumably angels) with God in heaven, and "ten thousand times ten thousand" (one-hundred million) figures (probably also angels) standing before Him.

• Isaiah 6:1-6 pictures angels hovering around God's throne, proclaiming, "Holy, holy, holy is the LORD Almighty" (verse 3).

• Jesus speaks of angels "ascending and descending" to and from heaven in John 1:51.

• Hebrews 12:22 exhorts believers, "You have come...to the city of the living God. You have come to thousands upon thousands of angels in joyful assembly."

• John the apostle, author of the Book of Revelation, said: "Then I looked and heard the voice of many angels, numbering thousands upon thousands, and ten thousand times ten thousand. They encircled the throne and the living creatures and the elders" (Revelation 5:11).

Believers Dwell in Heaven

A common theme of the Scriptures is that redeemed human beings will end up in the "Holy City" (Revelation 21:1-2; see also John 14:1-3; Colossians 1:12; Hebrews 11:16; 2 Peter 3:13), where we will reside forever. For this reason, the apostle Paul confidently asserts that "our citizenship is in heaven" (Philippians 3:20; see also Ephesians 2:19). We may be earthly citizens too, but in terms of our ultimate destiny, we are truly citizens of heaven. We are pilgrims passing through, on our way to another country, another land, another city. And we behave ourselves on earth as citizens of that future, glorious, eternal city.

Something we can all look forward to is that one day the voices of redeemed human beings will be joined with the voices of the angels in worship and praise to our eternal God. This glorious scene is described in detail in the Book of Revelation:

> After this I looked and there before me was a great multitude that no one could count, from every nation, tribe, people and language, standing before the throne and in front of the Lamb. They were wearing white robes and were holding palm branches in their hands. And they cried out in a loud voice: "Salvation belongs to our God, who sits on the throne, and to the Lamb." All the angels were standing round the throne and around the elders and the four living creatures. They fell down on their faces before the throne and worshiped God, saying: "Amen! Praise and glory and wisdom and thanks and honor and power and strength be to our God forever and ever. Amen!" (Revelation 7:9-12).

Do Animals (and Pets) Go to Heaven?

One of the most common questions I am asked about heaven and the afterlife is whether animals (or, more specifically, our pets) will be there. That's a tough question. I have had pets who have died and know how emotionally loaded this issue is. Some theologians seem quite sure that our pets will not be in heaven. Others, such as R.C. Sproul, have questioned that thinking. It is true that only human beings are created in the image of God (Genesis 1:26). Even though animals are not created in God's image, however, Sproul thinks it is possible that they may have souls. Here is what he says:

> Nowhere does Scripture explicitly state that animals do not have souls.... There's nothing in Scripture I know of that would preclude the possibility of animals' continued existence.... The Bible does give us some reason to hope that departed animals will be restored. We read in the Bible that redemption is a cosmic matter. The whole creation is destined to be redeemed through the work of Christ (Romans 8:21).[19]

There are many who would seem to agree with Sproul. Peter Kreeft asks, "Why not? How irrational is the prejudice that would allow plants (green fields and flowers) but not animals into heaven!"[20] He also asks, "Would the same animals be in heaven as on earth? Is my dead cat in heaven? Again, why not? God can raise up the very grass; why not cats?"[21] Mark Hitchcock, in agreement with Kreeft, suggests: "Revelation tells us that heaven will contain many of the same things that were in the original creation, such as a river, trees, and fruit. Why not animals too? After all, animals are an integral part of earthly life, and testify powerfully of the creative, imaginative genius of God. He created the giraffe, the camel, the platypus, the lion, the pachyderm, and the hummingbird."[22] C.S. Lewis speculated that redeemed humans will be "between the angels who are our elder brothers and the beasts who are our jesters, servants, and play fellows."[23]

Randy Alcorn suggests a number of reasons why animals might be in heaven. For example, God certainly went to great effort to save some animals during the time of Noah and the worldwide flood (Genesis 6:19-20). Moreover, Psalm 148 makes reference to all of creation rendering praise to God, including the animal kingdom: "Wild animals and all cattle, small creatures and flying birds...Let them praise the name of the LORD, for his name alone is exalted; his splendor is above the earth and the heavens" (verses 10,13). Psalm 150:6 likewise instructs, "Let everything that has breath praise the LORD." This would certainly include animals, since animals have breath. Elijah was taken up into heaven in a chariot pulled by horses (2 Kings 2:11), and heaven's army is said to ride on horses (Revelation 19:11-14). Finally, since animals (including the great behemoth and leviathan—Job 40–41) bring glory to God, why shouldn't animals be in heaven and on the new earth?[24]

How Many Redeemed Human Beings Will There Be in Heaven?

This issue has been debated throughout church history. The truth of the matter is that we cannot be sure regarding precisely how many will be saved and go to heaven. But there are some key considerations to keep in mind.

Some have held that very few ultimately make it to heaven. After all, Jesus Himself said, "Enter through the narrow gate. For wide is the gate and broad is the road that leads to destruction, and many enter through it. But small is the gate and narrow the road that leads to life, and *only a few find it*" (Matthew 7:13-14, emphasis added). Others have suggested, however, that this Scripture passage deals primarily with the *immediate* and *local* response to Jesus' message in New Testament times, not to people throughout human history. If this view is correct, then Matthew 7:13-14 should not be used as a gauge for how many people make it into heaven.

Christian apologist Norman Geisler suggests that the accumulative total of infants and children before the age of accountability who have died since the time of Adam and Eve must represent a significant portion of those who make it into heaven: "Granting that all who die in infancy go to heaven, that life begins at conception, and that the mortality rate before the age of accountability down through the millennia has been roughly half of those conceived, it would seem to follow that there will be more people saved than lost."[25]

Geisler also makes the keen observation that in terms of the accumulative total of the world's population since the time of Adam and Eve, many of those people are actually alive *in our own day* (since the world population has grown so geometrically in recent world history). It is therefore feasible that a great revival before Christ's return could bring many into the kingdom of God.[26]

All of this is simply to say that there could be far more people in heaven than anyone would initially think. Of course, regardless of how many actually end up in heaven, let us not forget that our all-loving God certainly *desires* that all be saved (2 Peter 3:9; 1 Timothy 2:4), although Scripture is clear that not all *will*, in fact, be saved (see Revelation 21:8). God offers salvation to all, but not all accept His invitation.

Does God Have a Throne Room in Heaven?

Yes, it would appear to be so. In Revelation 4:2-6 we read:

> There before me was a *throne in heaven with someone sitting on it.* And the one who sat there had the appearance of jasper and carnelian. A rainbow, resembling an emerald, encircled *the throne....* From *the throne* came flashes of lightning, rumblings and peals of thunder.... Also before *the throne* there was what looked like a sea of glass, clear as crystal (emphasis added).

Commenting on this verse, John MacArthur says that "language fails when men try to describe divine glory, so John is using these comparisons to precious jewels to picture the breathtaking beauty of heavenly glory. The jewels he mentions were the most stunning, glorious images he could picture, so he resorts to them to make his point."[27] God's throne room—like all of heaven—is clearly magnificent beyond description!

Does Satan Have Access to Heaven?

The primary occupants of heaven are God, angels, and redeemed human beings. However, based on events that took place in the book of Job, theologians also believe that Satan has the freedom to appear before God and engage in discourse with Him (see Job 1:6; 2:1). We are told in Revelation 12:10 that Satan is the "accuser of our brethren," which probably involves Satan going before God's throne and making slanderous statements and accusations about the saints (that's you and me). However, in the future Tribulation period, which precedes the second coming of Christ, Scripture indicates that the devil will be decisively cast out of heaven (Revelation 12:9). Sometime later he will be cast into the lake of fire, where he will spend the rest of eternity (Revelation 20:10). Satan's time is definitely limited.

What Are Some Things That Won't Be in Heaven?

There are quite a number of things that will not be in heaven. For example:

- There will be no temple—no separate building—to which one must go to encounter God's presence in heaven (Revelation 21:22). Scripture indicates that God is Himself (metaphorically) the temple in heaven.

- There will be no sea in heaven (Revelation 21:1). To some, the sea brings memories of the flood of Noah's time. To others, it can represent a great gulf of separation between loved ones (if they live on different sides of the ocean). Recall that as John wrote the Book of Revelation, he himself was isolated on the island of Patmos, surrounded by the sea, which kept him from those he loved in the churches throughout Asia Minor. A sealess heaven would mean no more exile or separation.[28]

• There will be no death in heaven (Revelation 21:4). The last enemy (death) will be forever gone, never again to raise its ugly head. No more funerals. Only life, life, and more life (1 Corinthians 15:54-55)!

• There will be no pain in heaven (Revelation 21:4). Heaven will involve an utterly pain-free existence. There will be no suffering of any kind—physical, emotional, spiritual, or other.

• There will be no crying or mourning or tears in heaven (Revelation 21:4)! There will be only endless joy, bliss, and serenity.

• There will be no night in heaven (Revelation 22:5). We will no longer have mortal bodies that need recuperation through sleep. Our resurrection bodies will never become fatigued. We will never become run-down.

• There will be no curse in heaven (Revelation 22:3), nor will there be any corruption. All will be perfect.

• There will be no satanic opposition in heaven (Revelation 20:10). Satan will be forever bound, never again free to harass the saints of the living God. His temptations toward evil, attempts to afflict us with bodily ailments, and seeds of doubt will be gone forever. Satan and his demons will be in eternal quarantine in hell.

What Do Children Think About Heaven?

Children have vivid, unrestrained imaginations—and that is something I love about them. Though children often have views that are biblically off-base, perhaps we adults nevertheless need to learn from them how to recover that sense of wonder that comes so naturally to them. Here is a representative sampling of how some young children view heaven:

- Michael, age 6, said of his house in heaven, "My house will be made out of Reese's Cups, and filled with chocolate."

- Sam, age 5, said, "No one dies, and no one cries, and everyone gets a lot of food."

- Ted, age 8, said, "I think heaven will have doors that have your name on it. When you open the door that has your name on it, there is a lot of fun stuff."

- Ben, age 9, said, "I think heaven looks like a giant forest with a golden path.... Diamonds will grow on trees! Trees will have faces, and so do mountains. There are flying ships and floating islands."

- Claire, age 10, said, "Heaven is nothing like Earth. There are no scary dreams, no thunderstorms, and no bullies. I imagine streets of gold, a beautiful landscape, high mountains, and fresh green valleys."

- Anna, age 9, waxed eloquent and had lots to say: "I will see my Grandpa running, happy and young. Little angels will be playing in fields. The gates will be made of pearls. You will never have to worry about cavities or what you eat. Maybe God's castle will be made out of tiny rose buds. There won't be any darkness. All the houses will be made out of rhinestones that shimmer. The picket fences won't be made out of wood but sun- flowers. There are flowers everywhere, some that you have seen and some that you have not seen." [29]

Though many such ideas are obviously quite unbiblical, it must surely bring a smile to the face of God to behold His young and immature little creatures saying such things. And surely it pleases Him to see the wonder and awe that His young creatures have for the future He has prepared for them! While I firmly believe we must be *biblical* in our view of heaven, I also believe that the more we understand what Scripture says about heaven and the afterlife, the greater will be that sense of childlike wonder and awe in our own hearts! So let us resolve to saturate our minds with all that Scripture teaches on this wondrous subject!

7

THE SPLENDOR OF THE
ETERNAL CITY:
THE NEW JERUSALEM

O ne of the greatest evangelists to ever grace this planet was Dwight Moody, a man who had an eternal perspective and did not fear what lay beyond death's door. He was excited about his heavenly destiny—living in the very presence of God.

The day Moody entered into glory is a day to remember:

> "Some day you will read in the papers that Dwight Moody is dead," the great evangelist exclaimed one hot Sunday in August 1899 to a New York City crowd. "Don't you believe a word of it! At that moment I shall be more alive than I am now.... I was born of the flesh in 1837; I was born of the Spirit in 1855. That which is born of the flesh may die. That which is born of the Spirit shall live forever."

> Four months later, exhausted from years of preach-
> ing and labor, Dwight Moody was dying. Early in
> the morning of December 22, Moody's son Will was
> startled by his father's voice from the bed across the
> room: "Earth recedes, heaven opens before me!"
>
> Will hurried to his father's side. "This is no dream,
> Will. It is beautiful.... If this is death, it is sweet. God
> is calling me and I must go. Don't call me back!"
>
> A few hours later Moody revived to find his wife and
> family gathered around him. He said to his wife, "I
> went to the gate of heaven. Why, it is so wonderful,
> and I saw the children [Irene and Dwight, who had
> died in childhood]." Within hours the man who had
> stirred two nations for Christ took a few final breaths
> and then entered the gate of heaven.[1]

Moody was caught up to heavenly paradise. The word "paradise" literally means "garden of pleasure" or "garden of delight."
Revelation 2:7 makes reference to heaven as the "paradise of God."
The apostle Paul said he "was caught up to paradise" and "heard
inexpressible things, things that man is not permitted to tell"
(2 Corinthians 12:4).

Apparently this paradise of God is so resplendently glorious,
so ineffable, so wondrous, that Paul was forbidden to say anything about it to those still in the earthly realm. But what Paul
saw instilled in him an eternal perspective that enabled him to
face the trials that lay ahead of him. He could hardly wait to get
back there (Philippians 1:21-23). This is where Moody went (and
where all Christians go) the moment their spirits depart the body
in death.

Moody's entry into glory is a perfect illustration of the fact
that Christ has taken the *sting* out of death for the Christian

(1 Corinthians 15:55; see also Isaiah 25:8; 2 Timothy 1:10; Revelation 21:4). The anticipation of entering heaven is altogether sweet for those who hold Christ dear to their hearts. So, dear saint, fear not that you will die. Your Savior has you in His hands in both life *and* death.

Today's Heaven Distinguished from the Future Heaven

Theologians and Bible expositors have been careful to distinguish between the *present* heaven where God now dwells and where believers go at the moment of death (2 Corinthians 5:8; Philippians 1:21-23) and the *future* heaven where believers will spend all eternity (2 Peter 3:13; Revelation 21:1). Previously in the book, I noted that God will one day create new heavens and a new earth. It is upon this new earth that the New Jerusalem, the heavenly city, will rest (Revelation 21:10). It will be this glorious city where you and I will reside for all eternity (see Revelation 21–22).

Christ Himself is the Builder of this city. We read Christ's own words in John 14:2-3: "In my Father's house are many rooms; if it were not so, I would have told you. I am going there to prepare a place for you. And if I go and prepare a place for you, I will come back and take you to be with me that you also may be where I am." You will see below that Jesus is quite the Architect! The place Jesus is preparing for us is glorious and wondrous, and has been the subject of inspiring hymns throughout church history. In one—"When We All Get to Heaven," written in the 1800s—we find the following lyrics that are worthy of meditation:

> Sing the wondrous love of Jesus,
> > Sing His mercy and His grace;
> In the mansions bright and blessed
> > He'll prepare for us a place.[2]

Putting Things into Perspective

You and I have such a limited perspective on this earth—this tiny little speck-of-a planet in a vast, seemingly endless universe. Sometimes when I go outside at night, I look up and see thousands of stars illuminating the sky. It boggles the mind to ponder that the same Christ who created all of this (John 1:3 ; Colossians 1:16) is the One who is the Builder of the place prepared for us in the Father's house (John 14:1-3).

To help put things into perspective, let us consider for a brief moment the magnitude of the stellar universe. Only about four thousand stars are visible to the human eye without a telescope. However, the creation's true vastness becomes evident when it is realized that with the giant telescopes now available, astronomers have estimated that there are about 10^{25} stars (that is, 10 million billion billion stars) in the known universe. Scientists estimate that this is about the number of grains of sand in the world.[3]

And who but God knows how many stars exist beyond the reach of our finite telescopes? As one Christian scholar put it, "Since God is infinite, and He is the Creator of the universe, there is no reason to assume that either our telescopes or our relativistic mathematics have penetrated to its boundaries."[4]

Not only is the grandeur of the created universe evident in the *number* of stars, but in their incredible *distances* from each other. Consider the following astounding facts about the vastness of the universe:

- The moon is only 211,453 miles away, and you could walk to it in twenty-seven years. A ray of light travels at 186,000 miles per second, so a beam of light would reach the moon in only one-and-a-half seconds.

- If we could travel at that speed, we would reach Venus

in two minutes and eighteen seconds because it's only 26 million miles away.

- After four-and-one-half minutes we would have passed Mercury, which is 50 million miles away.

- We could travel to Mars in four minutes and twenty-one seconds because it's only 34 million miles away.

- The next stop would be Jupiter—367 million miles away—and it would take us thirty-five minutes.

- Saturn is twice as far as Jupiter—790 million miles—and it would take one hour and eleven seconds.

- Eventually we would pass Uranus, Neptune, and finally Pluto—2.7 billion miles away. Having gotten that far, we still haven't left our solar system.

- The North Star is 400 hundred billion miles away, but that still isn't very far compared with known space.

- The star called Betelgeuse is 880 quadrillion miles from us and has a diameter of 250 million miles, which is greater than the earth's orbit around the sun.

- Where did it all come from? Who made it? It can't be an accident. Someone made it, and the Bible tells us it was Jesus Christ.[5]

Is not the stellar universe indescribably amazing? And is it not astounding to realize that Christ—the One who constructed this earth and the entire universe (John 1:3; Colossians 1:16; Hebrews 1:2)—is the Builder of the heavenly city in which we will dwell for all eternity? (John 14:1-3). I like the way Anne Graham Lotz put it:

Who created all the earthly beauty we have grown to love...the majestic snowcapped peaks of the Alps, the rushing mountain streams, the brilliantly colored fall leaves, the carpets of wildflowers, the glistening fin of a fish as it leaps out of a sparkling sea, the graceful gliding of a swan across the lake, the lilting notes of the canaries song, the whir of a hummingbird's wings, the shimmer of the dew on the grass in early morning...This is the same Creator who has prepared our heavenly home for us! If God could make the heavens and earth as beautiful as we think they are today—which includes thousands of years of wear and tear, corruption and pollution, sin and selfishness—can you imagine what the new heaven and the new earth will look like? It will be much more glorious than any eyes have seen, any ears have heard, or any minds have ever conceived.[6]

The New Jerusalem: A Real City

Perhaps the most elaborate description of the heavenly city contained in the Bible is Revelation 21, where we read all about the New Jerusalem. Randy Alcorn makes this interesting observation regarding what this *real* city might be like:

> Everyone knows what a city is—a place with buildings, streets, and residences occupied by people and subject to a common government. Cities have inhabitants, visitors, bustling activity, cultural events, and gatherings involving music, the arts, education, religion, entertainment, and athletics. If the capital city of the New Earth doesn't have these defining characteristics of a city, it would seem misleading for Scripture to repeatedly call it a city.[7]

That makes a lot of sense to me. You and I will have physically resurrected bodies—that is, *real* bodies. As *real* persons with *real* bodies, it is logical that we would forever live in a *real* city—the New Jerusalem (Revelation 21:2).

Indescribable, Simply Indescribable!

The description of the New Jerusalem—the heavenly city—in the Book of Revelation is astounding. Presented to our amazed gaze in Revelation 21 is a scene of such transcendent splendor that the human mind can scarcely take it in. This is a scene of ecstatic joy and fellowship of sinless angels and redeemed glorified human beings. The voice of the One identified as the Alpha and the Omega, the beginning and the end, utters a climactic declaration: "Behold, I am making all things new" (Revelation 21:5 NASB). J. Boudreau describes this glorious "new" city this way:

> What sublime descriptions the Holy Scriptures give us of the blessed City of God! Her walls are built of jasper-stone, but the city itself is of pure and shining gold, like unto clear crystal. And the foundations of the city are adorned with all manner of precious stones. Her gates are pearls. The very streets are transparent as glass. This glorious city has no need of the sun or of the moon to shine in her, for the glory of God is her light.[8]

Such words, based on the apostle John's own words in Revelation 21–22, no doubt represent a human attempt to describe the utterly indescribable. John F. Walvoord, the late president of Dallas Theological Seminary, observed that "the overall impression of the city as a gigantic brilliant jewel compared to jasper, clear as crystal, indicates its great beauty. John was trying to describe what he saw and to relate it to what might be familiar to his readers. However, it is evident that his revelation transcends anything that can be experienced."[9]

Theologian Millard Erickson agrees, and offers these reflections on the glorious splendor of this heavenly city: "Images suggesting immense size or brilliant light depict heaven as a place of unimaginable splendor, greatness, excellence, and beauty.... It is likely that while John's vision employs as metaphors those items which we think of as being most valuable and beautiful, the actual splendor of heaven far exceeds anything that we have yet experienced."[10]

George Marsden, author of *Jonathan Edwards: A Life,* points out that Edwards "recounted the similes used in Scripture to describe heaven," and that "his larger point was that, however wonderful it might be to imagine these things, earthly images are not really adequate.... These biblical images, he explained, are 'very faint shadows' that represent the joys of heaven humans are intended to enjoy."[11] In short, the heavenly city will be far more wondrous than we can possibly imagine.

One thing is certain. The city is designed to reflect and manifest the incredible glory of God. As Walvoord put it, "The constant mention of transparency indicates that the city is designed to transmit the glory of God in the form of light without hindrance."[12] The human imagination is simply incapable of fathoming the immeasurably resplendent glory of God that will be perpetually manifest in the eternal city. This is especially so when one considers the fact that all manner of precious stones will be built into the eternal city. Indeed, "this is a scene of indescribable beauty with the light of the city playing upon the multi-colored stones."[13]

Perfect in Every Way

Because you and I are so accustomed to living in a fallen world that has been viciously marred by sin and corruption, we find it impossible to conceive of what life might be like in a heavenly habitat that is *without* such sin and fallenness. From birth to death, we are confronted with imperfection on every level. But in the eternal city, we will experience *nothing but* perfection. I love the way A.T. Pierson has put it:

> There shall be no more curse—*perfect restoration.* The throne of God and of the Lamb shall be in it—*perfect administration.* His servants shall serve him—*perfect subordination.* And they shall see his face—*perfect transformation.* And his name shall be on their foreheads—*perfect identification.* And there shall be no night there; and they need no candle, neither light of the sun; for the Lord giveth them light—*perfect illumination.* And they shall reign forever and ever—*perfect exultation.*[14]

What could be better?

A *Huge* City

The heavenly city measures approximately 1500 miles by 1500 miles by 1500 miles. Though some interpret these big numbers symbolically, allegedly carrying the idea that "saved people are never crowded,"[15] I think the dimensions are intended to be interpreted literally.[16] The eternal city is so huge that it would measure approximately the distance "from Canada to Mexico, and from the Atlantic Ocean to the Rockies."[17] That is a surface area of 2.25 million square miles (by comparison, London is only 621 square miles).[18] Put another way, the ground level area of the city will be 15,000 times that of London.[19]

The city is tall enough that from the earth's surface it would reach about one-twentieth of the way to the moon.[20] If the city has stories, each being twelve feet high, then the city would have 600,000 stories.[21] *That is huge!*

A city which is that high might seem to present a formidable challenge to city travelers. We must not forget, however, that our resurrection bodies will likely have amazing capabilities. Some expositors believe our new bodies will have the ability to fly and get places *fast*. *That* would be very exciting!

Someone calculated that if this structure is cube-shaped, it would allow for 20 billion residents, each having his or her own private 75-acre cube.[22] If each residence were smaller, then there is room to accommodate 100 thousand billion people.[23] Even then, plenty of room is left over for parks, streets, and other things you would see in any normal city.

The eternal city could either be cube-shaped or pyramid-shaped—and there are good Christian scholars on both sides of the debate. Some prefer to consider it shaped as a pyramid, for this would explain how the river of the water of life could flow down the middle of the city's great street (Revelation 22:1-2). Others prefer to consider it shaped as a cube, for the holy of holies in Solomon's temple was cube-shaped (1 Kings 6:20), and hence a cubical shape of the New Jerusalem might be intended to communicate that this eternal city might be likened to a holy of holies throughout all eternity.[24]

High Walls and Open Gates

Revelation 21:12 tells us that the New Jerusalem has "a great, high wall with twelve gates, and with twelve angels at the gates. On the gates were written the names of the twelve tribes of Israel." Moreover, we are told, "the wall of the city had twelve foundations, and on them were the names of the twelve apostles of the Lamb" (Revelation 21:14).

Perhaps the angels are at each of the twelve gates not only as guardians but also in view of their role as ministering spirits to the heirs of salvation (Hebrews 1:14). Perhaps the names of the 12 tribes of Israel are written on the gates to remind us that "salvation is from the Jews" (John 4:22). And perhaps the names of the apostles appear on the foundations to remind us that the church was built upon these men of God (Ephesians 2:20). It is interesting to ponder what John's reaction might have been when he saw his own name inscribed on one of the foundations. What a thrill it must have been. It is like an eternal memorial to John's faithfulness—and the faithfulness of the other apostles—in defending the truth of Jesus Christ in an often-hostile world.

We might also note the view of some Bible expositors that "the inclusion of the names of the twelve tribes of Israel and the twelve apostles in the foundations and gates of the city indicates that both Jewish and Gentile believers will all be part of the family of God and share eternity as one."[25] The heavenly city includes the redeemed of all ages.

Notice that our text says of the eternal city that "on no day will its gates ever be shut, for there will be no night there" (Revelation 21:25). In ancient times, it was necessary to shut the gates of cities at night, else the city be overtaken by evil invaders during the night. Gates were part of the city's security. In the eternal city, however, there will never, ever be any external threat to those who dwell within. Satan, demons, and unbelievers will be in eternal quarantine in hell. Besides, God Himself will dwell within the city. Who would dare attack it?

A River, a Tree, and Healing Leaves

The "river of the water of life" has intrigued Bible interpreters since the first century. In Revelation 22:1 we read, "Then the angel showed me the river of the water of life, as clear as crystal, flowing from the throne of God and of the Lamb down the middle of the great street of the city."

Perhaps one of the best explanations is that this pure river of life, though it may be a real and material river, is nevertheless symbolic of the abundance of spiritual life that will characterize those who are living in the eternal city.[26] The stream seems to symbolize the perpetual outflow of spiritual blessing to all the redeemed of all ages, now basking in the full glow of eternal life. What spiritual blessedness there will be in the eternal state!

We next read of the Tree of Life (Revelation 22:2). It is interesting to observe that the last time we read of the Tree of Life was in Genesis 3, where Adam and Eve sinned in the Garden of Eden. Paradise was lost. Now, in the Book of Revelation, paradise is restored and we again witness the Tree of Life in the glorious eternal state.

The leaves on the tree are said to be for the healing of nations. But what does this mean? Will there actually be a *need* for healing, as if somehow things are not perfect in the eternal state? Albert Barnes suggests, "We are not to suppose that there will be sickness, and a healing process in heaven, for that idea is expressly excluded in Revelation 21:4"[27]—a verse which informs us that "there shall be no more death, neither sorrow, nor crying, neither shall there be any more pain: for the former things are passed away" (KJV). John Walvoord provides us with this helpful insight:

> The word for "healing" is *therapeia,* from which the English word therapeutic is derived, almost directly transliterated from the Greek. Rather than specifically meaning "healing," it should be understood as "health-giving," as the word in its root meaning has the idea of serving or ministering. In other words, the leaves of the tree promote the enjoyment of life in the New Jerusalem, and are not for correcting ills which do not exist.[28]

No Sun or Moon Needed

What is of great significance is the statement in Revelation 21:23 that "the city does not need the sun or the moon to shine on it, for the glory of God gives it light, and the Lamb is its lamp." This is in keeping with the prophecy in Isaiah 60:19: "The sun will no more be your light by day, nor will the brightness of the moon shine on you, for the LORD will be your everlasting light, and your God will be your glory."

Dr. Lehman Strauss's comments on the Lamb's glory are worthy of meditation:

> In that city which Christ has prepared for His own there will be no created light, simply because Christ Himself, who is the uncreated light (John 8:12), will be there...The created lights of God and of men are as darkness when compared with our Blessed Lord. The light He defuses throughout eternity is the unclouded, undimmed glory of His own Holy presence. In consequence of the fullness of that light, there shall be no night.[29]

A Holy City

In Revelation 21:1-2 we find heaven described as "the holy city." This is a fitting description. Indeed, in this city there will be no sin or unrighteousness of any kind. Only the pure of heart will dwell there.

This does not mean you and I must personally attain moral perfection in order to dwell there. Those of us who believe in Christ have been given the very righteousness of Christ (see Romans 4:11,22-24). Because Christ took our sins upon Himself at the cross for us, we have been *made* holy (Hebrews 10:14). Hence, we will have the privilege of living for all eternity in the Holy City.

Contrasting the New Jerusalem with Earth

As we read of John's description of the New Jerusalem, we find a whole series of contrasts with the earth. These contrasts have been wonderfully summarized by Bruce Shelley:

> In contrast to the darkness of most ancient cities, John says heaven is always lighted. In contrast to rampant disease in the ancient world, he says heaven has trees whose leaves heal all sorts of sicknesses. In contrast to the parched deserts of the Near East, he pictures heaven with an endless river of crystal-clear water. In contrast to a meager existence in an arid climate, John says twelve kinds of fruit grow on the trees of heaven. In a word, heaven is a wonderful destiny, free of the shortages and discomforts of this life.[30]

Finally, the purposes of God are fulfilled. God's plan of salvation, conceived in eternity past, is now brought into full fruition. And how glorious it will be. One of the great commentators of times past, Wilbur Smith, described it this way:

> All the glorious purposes of God, ordained from the foundation of the world, have now been attained. The rebellion of angels and mankind is finally subdued, as the King of kings assumes his rightful sovereignty. Absolute and unchangeable holiness characterizes all within the universal kingdom of God. The redeemed, made so by the blood of the Lamb, are in resurrection and eternal glory. Life is everywhere—and death will never intrude again. The earth and the heavens both are renewed. Light, beauty, holiness, joy, the presence of God, the worship of God, service to Christ, likeness to Christ—all are now abiding realities. The vocabulary of man, made for life here, is incapable of truly

and adequately depicting what God has prepared for those that love him.[31]

My friends, any way you look at it, the eternal city—the New Jerusalem—is going to be absolutely wonderful, far more so than any human mind could possibly fathom or even begin to imagine. Christians are merely pilgrims en route to the final frontier of the New Jerusalem, just "passing through" this brief "dot of time" on earth. We are wisest when we choose to daily follow the apostle Paul's advice in Colossians 3:1-2: "Set your hearts on things above, where Christ is seated at the right hand of God. Set your minds on things above, not on earthly things."

8

THE NEW HEAVENS
AND THE NEW EARTH

I n the previous chapter, I addressed the splendor of the eternal
city—the New Jerusalem. In the present chapter, I deal more
broadly with the new heavens and the new earth, upon which the
eternal city will one day come to rest (Revelation 21:2).

Think about it. In view of the sheer vastness of the stellar universe, it is truly amazing that God sovereignly chose our tiny
planet as a center of divine activity. Relatively speaking, the earth
is but an astronomical atom among the whirling constellations,
only a tiny speck of dust among the ocean of stars and planets
in the universe. To the naturalistic astronomer, the earth is but
one of many planets in our small solar system, all of which are in
orbit around the sun. But the earth is nevertheless the center of
God's work of salvation in the universe. For, indeed, it was on *the
earth* that God created humankind and has appeared to people

throughout biblical times. It was on *the earth* that Jesus became incarnate and died for the sins of humankind. It will be to *the earth* that the Lord Jesus comes again at the second coming. And He will then create the new heavens and a *new earth* (Revelation 21:1-2; 22:3).

The centrality of the earth is also evident in the creation account, for God created the earth before He created the rest of the planets and stars. Why did God create the sun, moon, and stars on the fourth day rather than the first day? Apparently because the earth is the central planet in God's sovereign plan.

Tragically, as we think back to the scene in the Garden of Eden in which Adam and Eve sinned against God, we remember that a curse was placed upon the earth by God (Genesis 3:17-18; see also Romans 8:20-22). Hence, before the eternal kingdom can be made manifest, God must deal with this cursed earth. We also remember that Satan has long carried out his evil schemes on earth (see Ephesians 2:2), and hence the earth must be purged of all stains resulting from his extended presence.[1] In short, then, the earth—along with the first and second heavens (the earth's atmosphere and the stellar universe)—must be renewed. The old must make room for the new.

The Scriptures often speak of the passing of the old heavens and earth. Psalm 102:25-26, for example, says that the earth and the stellar universe will perish, "but you [O God] remain; they will all wear out like a garment. Like clothing you will change them and they will be discarded."

In Isaiah 51:6 we likewise read, "Lift up your eyes to the heavens, look at the earth beneath; the heavens will vanish like smoke, the earth will wear out like a garment...But my salvation will last forever..." This reminds us of Jesus' words in Matthew 24:35, "Heaven and earth will pass away, but my words will never pass away."

Perhaps the most extended section of Scripture dealing with the passing of the old heavens and earth is 2 Peter 3:7-13:

> The present heavens and earth are reserved for fire, being kept for the day of judgment and destruction of ungodly men.... The heavens will disappear with a roar; the elements will be destroyed by fire, and the earth and everything in it will be laid bare. Since everything will be destroyed in this way, what kind of people ought you to be? You ought to live holy and godly lives as you look forward to the day of God and speed its coming. That day will bring about the destruction of the heavens by fire, and the elements will melt in the heat. But in keeping with his promise we are looking forward to a new heaven and a new earth, the home of righteousness.

After the universe is cleansed, and God creates a new heaven and a new earth, all vestiges of the curse and Satan's presence will be utterly and forever removed. As Albert Barnes has put it, "The earth will be no more cursed, and will produce no more thorns and thistles; man will be no more compelled to earn his bread by the sweat of his brow; woman will be no more doomed to bear the sufferings which she does now; and the abodes of the blessed will be no more cursed by sickness, sorrow, tears, and death."[2] John F. Walvoord adds "All that spoke of sin and its penalties is wiped away in heaven, and there is nothing left that is a reminder of sin. All are blessed, not cursed."[3] All things will be made new, and how blessed it will be!

An Expanded "Heaven"

Previously in the book, I noted that theologians and Bible expositors have been careful to distinguish between the *present* heaven where God now dwells and where believers go at the moment of death (2 Corinthians 5:8; Philippians 1:21-23) and the future heaven (2 Peter 3:13; Revelation 21:1) where believers will spend all eternity. For, indeed, a renovation is coming. As one expositor put it, "In the consummation of all things, God will renovate the heavens and the earth, merging His heaven with a new universe for a perfect dwelling-place that will be our home forever. In other words, heaven, the realm where God dwells, will expand to encompass the entire universe of creation, which will be fashioned into a perfect and glorious domain fit for the glory of heaven."[4] Peter speaks of this glorious future reality in 2 Peter 3:13. You and I can look forward to living eternally in a magnificent kingdom where both heaven and earth unite in a glory that exceeds the imaginative capabilities of the finite human brain.

Finally, the prophecy of Isaiah 65:17 will be fulfilled, where God promises: "Behold, I will create new heavens and a new earth. The former things will not be remembered, nor will they come to mind." *Finally*, the prophecy of Revelation 21:1-5 will be fulfilled: "Then I saw a new heaven and a new earth, for the first heaven and the first earth had passed away, and there was no longer any sea.... He who was seated on the throne said, 'I am making everything new!'" (Revelation 21:1-5).[5] My friends, rejoice! For we are destined for a new heaven and a new earth!

The Replacement View

Many Christians have wondered, In what sense are the earth and heavens made "new"? There are two primary viewpoints held by Christians—the *renewal* view and the *replacement* view.

The replacement view holds that the universe will be "annihilated and replaced with a brand new, second universe created *ex nihilo* ('out of nothing')."[6] In favor of this view are the statements in the Book of Revelation, "the first heaven and the first earth had *passed away,*" and "the old order of things have *passed away*" (21:1,4, emphasis added). (Other theologians point out, however, that such phrases could also be applicable to the renewal model, for Christians themselves are viewed as a "new creation" in which "the old has gone, the new has come" [2 Corinthians 5:17], phrases that seem to point to their spiritual *renewal,* not their *replacement.*) Another, perhaps more convincing argument offered in favor of the replacement view is Peter's affirmation that the present heavens and earth will be destroyed by fire (2 Peter 3:10-13).[7]

The Renewal View

According to the renewal view (my personal view), "the New Heavens and New Earth will be this present universe purified of all evil, sin, suffering, and death."[8] Bible scholars who hold to this view tell us that the Greek word used to designate the newness of the cosmos is not *neos* but *kainos. Neos* means "new in time" or "new in origin." But *kainos* means "new in nature" or "new in quality." Hence, the phrase "new heavens and a new earth" refers not to a cosmos that is totally other than the present cosmos. Rather, the new cosmos will stand in continuity with the present cosmos but will be utterly renewed and renovated.[9] As commentator William Hendrickson put it, "It is the same heaven and earth, but gloriously rejuvenated, with no weeds, thorns, or thistles."[10] J. Oswald Sanders likewise comments, "The picture is of the universe transformed, perfected, purged of everything that is evil and that exalts itself against God. It is 'new,' not in the sense of being a new creation, but of being new in character—a worthy milieu for the residents of God's redeemed people."[11]

This means that a *resurrected people* will live in a *resurrected universe!* As John Piper puts it, "What happens to our bodies and what happens to the creation go together. And what happens to our bodies is not annihilation but redemption.... Our bodies will be redeemed, restored, made new, not thrown away. And so it is with the heavens and the earth."[12]

Matthew 19:28 (NASB) thus speaks of "the regeneration" (see also Isaiah 65:18-25; Ezekiel 28:25-26; 34:25-30). The new heavens and earth, like our newness in Christ, will be regenerated, glorified, free from the curse of sin, and eternal. Acts 3:21 thus speaks of the "restoration of all things" (NASB). As Bible expositor Walter Scott put it, "Our planet will be put in the crucible, altered, changed, and made new, to abide forever."[13]

We can expect things to be on this new earth in continuity with the present earth—such as "atmosphere, mountains, water, trees, people, houses—even cities, buildings, and streets."[14] Randy Alcorn suggests that we pay careful attention to the words we find throughout the Bible: "Reconcile. Redeem. Restore. Recover. Return. Renew. Regenerate. Resurrect. Each of these biblical words begins with the re- prefix, suggesting a *return to an original condition* that was ruined or lost."[15] Just as many of Jesus' various miracles on earth involved *restoration* (such as restoration of health and/or life), so God's renewal of the universe will involve restoration.[16]

The new earth, being a renewed and an eternal earth, will be adapted to the vast moral and physical changes which the eternal state necessitates. Everything is new in the eternal state. Everything will be according to God's own glorious nature. The new heavens and the new earth will be brought into blessed conformity with all that God is—in a state of fixed bliss and absolute perfection.

Geological Changes

It seems clear that there will be geological changes in the new earth, for there will be no more sea (Revelation 21:1). At present about three-quarters of the earth's surface is covered with water and it is therefore uninhabitable. In the new earth, an immensely increased land surface will exist as a result of the disappearance of the oceans. Hence, as Albert Barnes observes, "the idea of John seems to be, the whole world will be inhabitable, and no part will be given up to the wastes of oceans."[17]

One Bible expositor suggests that while our present environment is water-based (our blood, for example, is 90 percent water), the environment in the new heavens and new earth will not be water-based, but will rather be based on a different life principle, a life principle that certainly includes the "water of life" (Revelation 22:1,17).[18] Again, then, glorified humanity will inhabit a glorified earth recreated and adapted to eternal conditions.

Heaven and Earth Merged

An incredible thing to ponder is that one day heaven and earth will no longer be separate realms, as they are now, but will be merged (I alluded to this previously). Believers will thus continue to be in heaven even while they are on the new earth.[19] The new earth will be utterly sinless, bathed and suffused in the light and splendor of God and unobscured by evil of any kind.

"Heaven" will thus encompass the new heaven and the new earth. And the New Jerusalem—the eternal city that measures 1500 by 1500 by 1500 miles—will apparently be "coming down" and resting upon the newly renovated earth (see Revelation 21:2). This city, as noted previously, will be the eternal dwelling place of the saints of all ages (see chapter 7).

How glorious the new heaven and the new earth will be. Even on our present earth, there are parts of the world untouched by human beings where one can behold the most glorious sunrise, and the scene is absolutely dazzling. Some days seem to have virtually perfect weather, allowing one to truly enjoy the world of nature.

And yet, the finest earth day shall be as nothing when compared with the new earth. For the new earth will be renovated to a state of absolute perfection—full of splendor and delight (1 Corinthians 2:9).

Sharing in Christ's Glory

As difficult as it may be to fully understand, the Scriptures indicate that in the eternal state—in the new heavens and the new earth—believers will actually share in the glory of Christ. Romans 8:17 tells us, "Now if we are children, then we are heirs—heirs of God and co-heirs with Christ, if indeed we share in his sufferings in order that we may also share in his glory." Likewise, Colossians 3:4 says, "When Christ, who is your life, appears, then you also will appear with him in glory."

This, of course, does not mean that finite humans become deity. But it does mean that you and I as Christians will be in a state of glory, sharing in Christ's glory, wholly because of what Christ has accomplished for us at the cross. We will have glorious resurrection bodies and be clothed with shining robes of immortality, incorruption, and splendor. And we will live in a perfect, glorious environment.

What About Our "Old" Families in the "New" World

Many Christians have wondered whether husbands and wives will *still be* husbands and wives in the new heavens and the new earth. It would seem from the scriptural evidence that believers will no longer be in a married state in the afterlife. The apostle Paul taught that marriage as a physical union is terminated at the death of either spouse (Romans 7:1-3; 1 Corinthians 7:39). Moreover, Jesus Himself said, "At the resurrection people will neither marry nor be given in marriage; they will be like the angels in heaven" (Matthew 22:30).

Of course, it will always be true that my wife, Kerri, and I were married on this earth. Nothing will ever change that. And in the eternal state, of the new heavens and the new earth, we will retain our memory that we were married on the old earth. It will be an eternal memory. And what a precious memory it will be. Moreover, I am quite certain that even though we will not be physically married, we will continue to grow in an ever-deepening and loving relationship with each other. As one pastor put it, couples who shared the closest intimacy on earth will no doubt continue to know, treasure, and appreciate each other throughout all eternity in heaven.[20]

Contrary to the teaching of some modern Christian writers,[21] I do not believe that married Christians will continue to engage in sex in heaven. We will be similar to the angels in the sense of not being married (Matthew 22:30), procreating, or sharing sexual intimacy. I believe we are most accurate biblically when we banish from our ideas of heaven the various carnal and sensual pleasures of the present world. Such pleasures, which were intended only for this world of imperfection, will be replaced by others of a far superior nature.[22] I believe John MacArthur is correct when he suggests,

> Here on earth man needs a helper, woman needs a protector, and God has designed both to produce children. In heaven, man will no longer require a helper because he will be perfect. Woman will no longer need a protector because she will be perfect. And the population of heaven will be fixed. Thus marriage as an institution will be unnecessary.[23]

We should not think of this as a deprivation. It may be very difficult for us to conceive how we could be happy and fulfilled in heaven without being married to our present spouse or having any more sexual relations. But God Himself has promised that not only will there *not* be any sense of deprivation, there will be only bliss, and there will be no more sorrow or pain.

My wife, Kerri, and I are part of the glorious church, which, the Scriptures reveal, will one day be married to Christ. This event is referred to as the marriage of the Lamb (Revelation 19:7-9). It is an event to look forward to with great anticipation.

What about our children? Will they *still* be our children in the afterlife? *Of course they will!* It will always be true that your daughter is your daughter and your son is your son. Receiving a glorified body does not obliterate the fact that in earth-time history a husband and wife conceived and gave birth to a son or daughter.

In the eternal state, however, there is a broader relationship in which we are all equally "sons" and "daughters" in God's eternal family. We have each become adopted into His forever family (Ephesians 1:5) for all eternity. And the one thing you can count on is that we will actually have deeper and more fulfilling relationships with our loved ones in heaven.

So, my friend, be encouraged! A glorious future awaits each of us. We will one day have perfect, glorious bodies in a perfect, glorious environment—the new heavens and the new earth. Nothing that life throws at us in the present stands a chance of overcoming our joy over the future! Stay strong in your faith!

It Is Done!

In Revelation 21:6 God victoriously pronounces, "It is done." This is truly a statement of divine finality. It represents a promise from God Almighty that what He has created for humankind's eternal state will indeed last forever and ever.[24] Just as Jesus Himself uttered the words "It is finished" in regard to completing His redemptive work upon the cross (John 19:30), so now God affirms that human salvation has now come to full fruition in the eternal state. As one expositor put it, "The great work is accomplished; the arrangement of human affairs is complete. The redeemed are gathered in; the wicked are cut off; truth is triumphant, and all is now complete—prepared for the eternal state of things."[25]

9

THE BLESSING OF
HEAVEN FOR BELIEVERS

In a general sense, I have already demonstrated that heaven holds many blessings in store for those who trust in Jesus Christ. Scripture repeatedly indicates that heaven is a realm of unsurpassed joy, unfading glory, undiminished bliss, unlimited delights, and unending pleasures. In what follows, I will zero in on specific blessings.

As we explore what Scripture says about the blessing of heaven for believers, keep ever before your mind what this information means *to you personally*. Heaven is not just a doctrine. Our forward gaze of heaven has everything to do with how we live as Christians in the present.

The Absence of Death

The Old Testament promises that in the heavenly state death will be swallowed up forever (Isaiah 25:8). This is somewhat of a

Hebrew play on words. The ancient Hebrews believed that death had a nasty habit of swallowing up the living. But here it is promised that things will be reversed—that is, the heavenly state will forever swallow up death, so that it becomes a thing of the past.

Paul speaks of this same reality as it relates to the future resurrection: "When the perishable has been clothed with the imperishable, and the mortal with immortality, then the saying that is written will come true: 'Death has been swallowed up in victory'" (1 Corinthians 15:54). Revelation 21:4 likewise tells us that God "will wipe every tear from their eyes. There will be no more death or mourning or crying or pain, for the old order of things has passed away." As one saint of days past put it, "There shall be no more disease and weakness and decay; the coffin, and the funeral, and the grave, and the dark-black mourning shall be things unknown."[1] And another has written:

> In all that future world of glory, not one shall ever die; not a grave shall ever be dug! What a view do we begin to get of heaven, when we are told there shall be no death there! How different from earth, where death is so common; where it spares no one; where our best friends die; where the wise, the good, the useful, the lovely, die; where fathers, mothers, wives, husbands, sons, daughters, all die; where we habitually feel that we must die. Assuredly we have here a view of heaven most glorious and animating to those who dwell in a world like this, and to whom nothing is more common than death.[2]

What an awesome blessing this is: There will be *no more death*—no more fatal accidents, no more incurable diseases, no more funeral services, no more final farewells. Death will be gone and done with, never again to be faced by those who dwell in heaven. Life in the eternal city will be painless, tearless, and deathless.

No More Mourning

In biblical times, mourning over someone's death was not just an individual matter involving private tears. Rather, the ancient Israelites made a very big show of their grief. There would typically be loud weeping and wailing, mourners would put ashes on their heads, they would tear their clothing in grief, they would walk barefoot, shave their beards off, and much more. In many cases, professional mourners would be hired to add to the loud wailing. The traditional time of mourning was seven days, but people may have mourned for an important person much longer. While people today do not typically express mourning so publicly or extravagantly, mourning is still very much a part of the human race because death is still very much a part of the human race.

Revelation 21:4, however, absolutely promises: "He will wipe every tear from their eyes. There will be no more death or mourning or crying or pain, for the old order of things has passed away." Revelation 7:17 likewise asserts that "God will wipe away every tear from their eyes" (see also Isaiah 25:8). It is noteworthy that in the original Greek of this verse, it says not *tears* (in a general sense) but *every tear* (singular), as if God will wipe away *every single tear* of *every single believer*.[3] Albert Barnes reflects, "How innumerable are the sources of sorrow here; how constant is it on the earth!...How different, therefore, will heaven be when we shall have the assurance that henceforward grief shall be at an end!"[4] Not a single tear will be upon our faces!

Let us be careful to observe that it is not that we will be sad in heaven and need to be cheered. John Walvoord is correct in his view that in making this statement about wiping every tear, "the revelation does not mean that we will start crying in heaven and

144   THE WONDER OF HEAVEN

then have our crying eased, but, rather, it will be foreign to the whole setting. It will be a time of rejoicing in the grace of God…"[5] In short, there will be nothing to cry about!

Try to imagine it—no mourning, no crying, no pain! *Ever!* One Bible expositor mused, "There will be no tears of regret, tears over the death of loved ones, or tears for any other reason."[6] This is a wondrous future to contemplate.[7]

As we ponder this future, it is well to observe that tears, pain, sorrow, and death entered the human race following the fall of Adam and Eve. One only need read the book of Genesis and the books that follow to see that this is so. In heaven, however, the effects of the curse will be utterly reversed so that tears, pain, sorrow, and death are a thing of the distant past. *All things are made new!*[8]

How Can We Be Happy if People Are Suffering in Hell?

Some have raised the question about how the saints in heaven can be happy, with no tears or mourning, if they are aware of people—especially loved ones—who are suffering in hell. Admittedly, this is a difficult question to answer. In fact, on this side of eternity, we do not have all the wisdom and insight we need to fully answer it. But there are some scriptural considerations that help us keep this question in perspective.

First, it is the conclusion of some theologians that God may purge the memories of the saints in heaven so that they do not personally have memories of those who are now in hell. As one Christian leader put it, "God may erase memories of a wayward son from the mind of his mother so that she may enjoy the full bliss of heaven unaware that she even had the son who is now damned."[9] Isaiah 65:17-19, where God speaks of the new heavens and a new earth, is cited in support of this viewpoint: "Behold, I will create new heavens and a new earth. *The former things will not be remembered, nor will they come to mind*...the sound of weeping and of crying will be heard in it no more" (emphasis added). While it is entirely possible that God may purge *some* memories, Bible expositor John MacArthur is careful to point out that

> this cannot possibly mean we will forget *everything* about this earth and our life and relationships here. After all, we will continue many of those same relationships eternally. And we will spend eternity reciting the glory of how Christ has redeemed us. Since our redemption was accomplished by His work on earth, it is impossible that we will completely lose our memory of *all* earthly events and relationships.[10]

What this means, then, is that God may *selectively* purge only those memories relating to people who spend eternity in hell. Such purging might be viewed as an act of grace and mercy on behalf of the saints in heaven.

Second, while it is possible that God may selectively purge some memories, even if God *does not* purge memories Scripture asserts that God Himself has promised that *He Himself* will take away all pain and remove all our tears (Revelation 21:4). It is in *His* hands. It is *His* responsibility. We may not be fully aware of how He will do it, but we can rest assured that God has the power and ability to do as He has promised. It is a *concrete fact* that we will be *serenely happy* in heaven. God has promised it and He will bring it about.

Third, in the heavenly state we will each be aware of the full justice of all of God's decisions. We will clearly see that those who are in hell are there precisely because they rejected God's only provision for escaping hell, choosing instead the path of sin, suffering, and death. Pastor Mark Hitchcock notes that, "in heaven we will have a perfected spirit with an ability to see things clearly from the divine perspective."[11] So, while God may selectively purge some of our specific individual memories, we will also be aware (without necessarily knowing specific identities) that any people who are in hell are there because they deserve it.

Fourth, we will have a sense of God's perfect justice in the recognition that there are degrees of punishment in hell (Matthew 10:15). This gives us an assurance that the Hitlers of human history will be in a much greater state of suffering than, for example, a non-Christian moralist. God is perfectly wise and just. He knows what He is doing! You and I can rest with quiet assurance in God's wisdom and justice when it comes to judging unbelievers.

Ultimately, we have to take God at His Word. He has promised there will be no more mourning, pain, or tears in heaven. We may not fully fathom how He will bring that condition about, but we can surely trust that He will do it.

Intimate Fellowship with God and Christ

In times past, God made His presence known in a variety of ways. He appeared to the patriarchs in the form of "the angel of the LORD" (Genesis 22:11-15). He appeared to Moses in a burning bush (Exodus 3:2). When God delivered the Israelites from Egyptian bondage, and they were traveling in the wilderness, we are told, "By day the LORD went ahead of them in a pillar of cloud to guide them on their way and by night in a pillar of fire to give them light, so that they could travel by day or night" (Exodus 13:21). In New Testament times, God was uniquely revealed in the person of Jesus Christ (John 1:1,14,18). In our day, God's presence is manifest to us through the power of the Holy Spirit (John 14–16). But on that future day, in the glorious eternal state, we will finally have unhindered, full access to God and will behold Him face-to-face.[12]

Indeed, John declared that in heaven, "They will *see his face*" (Revelation 22:4). The apostle Paul affirmed, "Now we see but a poor reflection as in a mirror; then *we shall see face to face*. Now I know in part; then I shall know fully, even as I am fully known" (1 Corinthians 13:12). The psalmist added: "And I…*I shall see your face*" (Psalm 17:15). John also said, "We know that when he appears, we shall be like him, for *we shall see him as he is*" (1 John 3:2, emphasis added in preceding verses).

Can there be anything more utterly sublime and satisfying for the Christian than to enjoy the sheer delight of unbroken fellowship with God, and have immediate and completely unobstructed access to the divine glory (John 14:3, 2 Corinthians 5:6-8, Philippians 1:23, 1 Thessalonians 4:17)? We shall see him "face to face," as it were, in all His splendor and glory.[13] We will gaze upon His countenance and behold His resplendent beauty forever.

Surely there can be no greater joy or exhilarating thrill for the creature than to look upon the face of the divine Creator and fellowship with Him forever. He "who alone possesses immortality and dwells in unapproachable light" (1 Timothy 6:16 NASB) shall reside intimately among His own, and "they shall be His people, and God Himself shall be among them" (Revelation 21:3 NASB). No wonder the psalmist exulted, "You will fill me with joy in your presence, with eternal pleasures at your right hand" (Psalm 16:11).

In the afterlife there will no longer be intermittent fellowship with the Lord, blighted by sin and defeat. Instead, it will be continuous. For believers, the sin problem will no longer exist. When we enter into glory we will no longer have the sin nature within us. Sin will be banished from our very being. All things will be made new!

To fellowship with God is the essence of heavenly life, the fount and source of all blessing. We may be confident that the crowning wonder of our experience in the eternal city will be the perpetual and endless exploration of that unutterable beauty, majesty, love, holiness, power, joy, and grace which is God Himself.[14]

Revelation 21:3 assures us, "Now the dwelling of God is with men, and he will live with them. They will be his people, and God himself will be with them and be their God." God in His infinite holiness will dwell among redeemed human beings, because Adam's curse will have been removed, Satan and the fallen angels will have been judged, the wicked will have been punished and quarantined from God, and the universe will have been made sinless (Revelation 20:15; 21:8; 22:15).

This brings to my mind the fact that when our beloved Christ was born on earth, He was called Immanuel, which means "God with us" (see Matthew 1:23). Throughout the entire eternal state, Jesus will be "with us" is the closest possible sense, "face to face" (1 Corinthians 13:12; see Revelation 22:4).

In that wonderful hymn, "Face to Face with Christ, My Savior," we read words worthy of meditation:

> Face to face with Christ, my Savior,
> Face to face, what will it be?
> When with rapture I behold Him,
> Jesus Christ who died for me.
>
> Face to face! O blissful moment!
> Face to face, to see and know;
> Face to face with my Redeemer,
> Jesus Christ who loves me so.
>
> Face to face I shall behold Him,
> Far beyond the starry sky.
> Face to face in all His glory,
> I shall see Him by and by.[15]

Some theologians speak of "the Beatific Vision" when addressing the wondrous reality that we will be in the direct presence of God throughout the rest of eternity. The term comes from three Latin words that carry the meaning "a happy-making sight." The idea is that the very beholding of God is something that brings perpetual happiness and joy. Randy Alcorn says that "our primary joy in Heaven will be knowing and seeing God."[16] Barry Morrow suggests that "this contemplation of God will not be a static, boring experience of simply staring at God but rather a dynamic, unending exploration of God and His attributes."[17] Because God is infinitely perfect in His attributes, one could spend an eternity contemplating them.

Reunion with Christian Loved Ones and Friends

One of most glorious aspects of our endless existence in heaven is that we will be forever reunited with Christian loved ones and friends. I love the way J.C. Ryle describes this reunion:

> Our pleasant communion with our kind Christian friends is only broken off for a small moment, and is soon to be eternally resumed. These eyes of ours shall once more look upon their faces, and these ears of ours shall once more hear them speak.... Blessed and happy indeed will that meeting be—better a thousand times than the parting! We parted in sorrow, and we shall meet in joy; we parted in stormy weather, and we shall meet in a calm harbor; we parted amidst pains and aches, and groans and infirmities: we shall meet with glorious bodies, able to serve our Lord forever without distraction.[18]

How do we know we will be reunited with Christian loved ones and friends? Scripture abounds with inspiring evidences.

The Thessalonian Christians were apparently very concerned about their Christian loved ones and friends who had died. They expressed their concern to the apostle Paul. So, in 1 Thessalonians 4:13-17, Paul speaks about the "dead in Christ" and assures the Thessalonian Christians that there will indeed be a reunion in heaven. Certainly the apostle Paul expected to be with his beloved Thessalonian friends in heaven, for we read in 1 Thessalonians 2:19: "What is our hope, our joy, or the crown in which we will glory in the presence of our Lord Jesus when he comes? *Is it not you?*" Paul rejoiced at the thought that he would be with his Thessalonian friends face-to-face in heaven.

Scripture is also clear that believers will *recognize* their loved ones and friends in the afterlife. First and foremost is the fact that the disciples recognized Jesus in His postresurrection appearances to them (for example, John 20:26-29)—a fact which implies that we too will recognize one another. We add to this the clear teaching of 1 Thessalonians 4:13-17, which speaks of a heavenly reunion of Christian loved ones and friends, something that obviously demands recognition of each other. (What good is a reunion if no one recognizes each other?) Moreover, we are told in 2 Samuel 12:23 that David knew he would be reunited with his deceased son in heaven. He had no doubt about recognizing him. As well, when Moses and Elijah (both of whom had long passed from earthly life) appeared to Jesus on the Mount of Transfiguration (Matthew 17:1-8), they were recognized by all who were present. Furthermore, in Jesus' story of the rich man and Lazarus in the afterlife (Luke 16:19-31), the rich man, Lazarus, and Abraham all recognized each other.

Still further, 1 Corinthians 13:12 tells us, "Now we see but a poor reflection as in a mirror; then we shall see face to face. Now I know in part; then I shall know fully, even as I am fully known." The mirrors of the ancients were made of polished metal and were far inferior to the mirrors we have today. The images were dark and indistinct. Similarly, our present knowledge is but a faint reflection of the fullness of knowledge we will have in the afterlife. This being so, we shall surely recognize our Christian loved ones and friends in the eternal state.

A thought worthy of pondering is not only that we will be reconciled with Christian loved ones and friends in heaven, and *recognize* them, but our relationships with them will be utterly perfect. Here on fallen earth, we fall into disagreements and sometimes fight with those whom we love. In heaven, such things will be gone forever. There will be no more cross words, no more misunderstandings, no more neglect shown to people, no rivalries, no jealousies, no competing for someone's love, and no selfishness. Our relationships in heaven will truly be wonderful and utterly satisfying.[19]

I have one further thought to share with you on this. Many of us have lost loved ones whom we are sure are in heaven. Because we love them so much, we yearn to be with them. But think about it for a moment. Knowing that they are now in a state in which they have no mourning, no tears, no pain, no more fear of death, and are enjoying direct and serene fellowship with Christ, *dare we even contemplate wishing them back here on sinful earth?* Banish the idea from your mind! Love compels us to seek their highest good, and their highest good is found only in heaven. We will join them soon enough!

Satisfaction of All Needs and Perfect Rest

In our present life on earth, there are times when we go hungry and thirsty. There are times when our needs are not met. In the eternal state, however, God will abundantly meet each and every need.

Revelation 7:16-17 promises, "Never again will they hunger; never again will they thirst. The sun will not beat upon them, nor any scorching heat. For the Lamb at the center of the throne will be their shepherd; he will lead them to springs of living water. And God will wipe away every tear from their eyes."

The Scriptures also indicate that a key feature of heavenly life is rest (Revelation 14:13). No more deadlines to work toward. No more overtime work in order to make ends meet. No more breaking one's back. Just rest. *Sweet serene rest.* And our rest will be especially sweet since it is ultimately a rest in the very presence of God, who meets our every need. As the Puritan writer Richard Baxter put it in his classic book *Saints' Everlasting Rest,* "This rest will be absolutely perfect. We shall then have joy without sorrow, and rest without weariness." Indeed, "the saints' rest is the most happy state of the Christian" and is "the perfect, endless enjoyment of God."[20] We will one day find ourselves in a state in which "no selfish thought, no unkind or impure motive, no wrong desire, ever clouds the mind; where no anxiety ever disturbs one's deep heart-rest; where no temptation ever shoots its gilded but poisoned arrows; where no suffering or sorrow ever rends one's spirit; and where no jarring discord of any kind ever sounds amid the deep, rich harmonies of a sinless society."[21]

Activities of Believers in Heaven

What will we do for all eternity in heaven? Will we be sitting on clouds playing harps?

Not by any means! There will be no purposeless inactivity in the eternal state. Scripture portrays believers as being involved in meaningful—*and yet restful*—service throughout eternity. Let's take a brief look at just a few of the things believers will spend their time doing in the eternal state.

Praising and Worshiping God and Christ

The Book of Revelation portrays believers in the eternal state as offering worship and praise before the throne of God and Christ. The Hebrew word for worship, *shakha,* means "to bow down" or "to prostrate oneself" (see Genesis 22:5; 42:6). Likewise, the New Testament word for worship, *proskuneo,* means "to prostrate oneself" (see Matthew 2:2,8,11). In Old English, "worship" was rendered "worthship," pointing to the worthiness of the God we worship. Such worship is the proper response of a creature to the divine Creator (Psalm 95:6).

Scripture tells us that some angels unceasingly worship God day and night. Revelation 4:8, for example, tells us, "Each of the four living creatures [angels] had six wings and was covered with eyes all around, even under his wings. Day and night they never stop saying: 'Holy, holy, holy is the Lord God Almighty, who was, and is, and is to come.'" Scripture gives the distinct impression that the angels give this praise audibly, as they did at the birth of Jesus Christ (Luke 2:13-14). The apostle John speaks of 100 million angels singing praises in unison to the God they adore:

> Then I looked and heard the voice of many angels, numbering thousands upon thousands, and ten thousand times ten thousand. They encircled the throne and the living creatures and the elders. In a loud voice they sang: "Worthy is the Lamb, who was slain, to receive power and wealth and wisdom and strength and honor and glory and praise!" (Revelation 5:11-12).

Someday, glorified believers will join in the company of angels in singing praise and rendering worship to God. In Revelation 7:9-10, we read of a great multitude of believers before God's throne worshipfully crying out, "Salvation belongs to our God, who sits on the throne, and to the Lamb." Revelation 19:1-6 portrays a

great multitude of believers worshipfully shouting out, "Hallelujah" before God's throne. This is something every believer can
look forward to.

   The worship that takes place in heaven will be ultimately fulfilling. I like the way Joni Eareckson Tada puts it: "Praise will
not be something we will be assigned or commanded to do; it
will be natural." She says it will be "a supernatural effervescent
response of the born-again creature, new and fit for heaven."[22]
Pastor Douglas Connelly concurs: "Heavenly worship will not
be confining or manipulative, but spontaneous and genuine…
We will lose ourselves in the sheer joy of expressing with our lips
the adoration and love we feel for God in our hearts…You won't
find quiet, solemn worship clothed in hushed tones and organ
music either. Instead you will hear shouts and loud voices and
trumpets."[23]

Serving God and Christ

   Scripture indicates that while we will be busy in our service
to God (Revelation 1:5-6), this service will not be toilsome or
draining, but invigorating and fulfilling. It will not be *tedious*
service but *joyous* service—fully meeting our heart's every desire.
We will find immeasurable satisfaction in our service to God. As
Christian scholars Thomas Ice and Timothy Demy put it, "Service
to God in heaven will be without time demands, without frustration, without fear of failure, without limitations, and without
exhaustion. It will come from worship and motivation that is
pure, and it will be a joyful experience."[24]

   Based on Jesus' parable in Luke 19:11-27, it would seem that
one factor that relates to our service in the eternal state is faithfulness in serving Christ during our mortal state on earth. In the
parable the master affirmed to one of the servants, "Because you
have been trustworthy in a very small matter, take charge of ten

cities" (verse 17). The idea seems to be that if we are faithful in this life, Christ will entrust us with more in serving Him in the next life.

It would seem that one aspect of our service will involve reigning with Christ. In Revelation 22:5 we are told that believers—God's faithful bondservants—"will reign for ever and ever" (see also Revelation 5:10). God's faithful believers will be involved in some capacity in the heavenly government.*

Part of our service will also involve judging the angels in some capacity: "Do you not know that we will judge angels?" (1 Corinthians 6:2-3). This is noteworthy because humanity at present is lower than the "heavenly beings" (angels—see Psalm 8). The situation will be reversed in the eternal state. Angels will be lower than redeemed human beings in heaven.

Believers will be serving God in the heavenly "temple as well." Indeed, the Book of Revelation tells us that believers "are before the throne of God and serve him day and night in his temple" (Revelation 7:15). Bible expositors are careful to point out, however, that the reference to "temple" in this verse is a metaphorical way of describing God's presence. After all, Revelation 21:22 tells us that there is no *actual* temple in the eternal city, for the Lord God and the Lamb *are* the temple. Hence, to serve God "day and night in his temple" refers to perpetually serving God in His very presence. *Glorious!*

Learning More About Our Incomparable God

We will apparently be able to grow in knowledge in our heavenly existence. Throughout future ages believers will be shown "the incomparable riches of his grace" (Ephesians 2:7). Though our capacity for knowledge and our actual intelligence

---

* Some Christians believe the privilege of reigning with Christ belongs only to faithful and overcoming Christians (see, for example, Revelation 2:26), not uncommitted Christians.

will be greatly increased and expanded (1 Corinthians 13:12), we will not be omniscient (all-knowing). Only God is omniscient (omniscience is one of the *incommunicable* attributes of God). We will forever maintain our capacity to learn as finite beings.[25] Even now, the angels continue to learn about God and His ways (1 Peter 1:12).

This means that redeemed humans will never get bored in heaven. God is so infinite—with matchless perfections that are beyond us in every way—that we will never come to the end of exploring Him and His marvelous riches. For all eternity we will always be learning and discovering more about the wonders and majesty of our great God and His creation. As one theologian puts it,

> We will constantly be more amazed with God, more in love with God, and thus ever more relishing his presence and our relationship with him. Our experience of God will never reach its consummation. We will never finally arrive, as if upon reaching a peak we discover there is nothing beyond. Our experience of God will never become stale. It will deepen and develop, intensify and amplify, unfold and increase, broaden and balloon.[26]

Fellowship with Believers We've Never Met

One fabulous thing we can all look forward to is that in heaven we will be able to enjoy fellowship with believers we've never met before—including those mentioned in the Bible as well as famous believers throughout human history. We will get to spend quality time with Noah, Abraham, Isaac, Jacob, Joseph, Moses, Joshua, David, Esther, Elijah, Elisha, Isaiah, Ezekiel, Daniel, Matthew, Mark, Luke, John, Mary, Paul, Peter, and all the other notable saints of biblical times. We'll get to ask them about some of their biblical "moments," such as when Moses parted the sea, or when David slew Goliath, or when Peter sank when trying to walk on water, or when the thief on the cross was promised paradise by Christ. We will get to spend time with Augustine, Martin Luther, John Calvin, John Wesley, Charles Wesley, C.S. Lewis, Dwight L. Moody, and so many others. Not only that, but we will also have the chance to meet and get to know believers from every age that we've never met and never even heard of. *What delightful fellowship all of this will be!*

Things We *Won't* Do in Heaven

Just as Scripture is clear about some of the things we will be doing in heaven for all eternity, Scripture is also clear about some things we will never do in heaven throughout all eternity. I like what Mark Hitchcock says about this: "We will never sin, never make mistakes, never need to confess, never have to repair or replace things (no leaky faucets, no changing light bulbs, no car repairs). We will never have to…defend ourselves, apologize, experience guilt, battle with Satan or demons…or experience… rehabilitation, loneliness, depression, or fatigue."[27]

Especially wonderful is the fact that sin will be a thing of the past, never again to rear its ugly head to cause us problems. Romans 6:23 tells us that "the wages of sin is death," but in heaven there "will be no more death" (Revelation 21:4). There will only be *life*—and a perfect life, at that! As the puritan preacher Jonathan Edwards put it, "There shall be no pollution or deformity or offensive defect of any kind, seen in any person or thing; but everyone shall be perfectly pure, and perfectly lovely in heaven."[28]

The absence of all these negative things will contribute immensely to our sense of joy and well-being in heaven. Indeed, "heaven is the eternal presence of everything that can make a saint happy, and the eternal absence of everything that can cause sorrow."[29] Never again will we have to deal with or even think about sickness, pain, disease, death, poverty, misunderstanding, slander, lying, strife, contention, quarrels, envies, jealousies, bad tempers, infidelity, skepticism, wars, fighting, bloodshed, murderers, or lawsuits. All such things will be eternally banished in heaven.[30]

Oh, the Wonder!

Oh, the wonder of what awaits each of us in the afterlife. Oh, the wonder of perfect bodies. Oh, the wonder of a perfect environment. Oh, the wonder of no more death, no more sin, no more pain, no more mourning, and no more Satan. Oh, the wonder of what God has prepared for us. *Praise His name!*

10

HEAVEN FOR THOSE
WHO CAN'T BELIEVE

There is perhaps nothing more difficult in the world than for a parent to bury a child. How heart wrenching it is for a mother and father to watch as the casket containing their beloved son or daughter is lowered into the ground.

Understandably, an issue of great concern to Christian parents relates to the eternal status of those who die in infancy or early childhood. Infants, toddlers, and most little children obviously do not have the capacity to "believe" in Jesus Christ for salvation. The same may be said of some mentally handicapped people. They simply do not have the mental ability to place saving faith in Jesus. So, what about heaven for those who cannot believe? What do the Scriptures—the fountain of truth—teach?

Throughout the centuries various theories on this issue have been suggested by Christian thinkers.[1] Some have argued that infants are sinless and morally innocent, and hence are automatically saved if they should die. However, this view goes against the clear scriptural teaching that all human beings are born with a sin nature (Psalm 14:1; Romans 3:23; 5:12; James 3:2; 1 John 1:8-10; more on this below).

Others have focused their entire attention on the love of God. Since God is a God of love, it is argued, He would not send an infant to hell. While this view correctly recognizes God's love (1 John 4:8), it ignores God's other attributes—such as His holiness (1 Peter 1:16). God does not violate His holy standards in order to show love. God never "lovingly" overlooks the sin nature of any human being (including infants).

Still others have argued that God by His foreknowledge looks down into the hypothetical future of the deceased child to determine whether or not he or she *would have* believed in Jesus. Those who would have believed are deemed saved. Those who would not have believed are deemed unsaved.

All of these viewpoints have serious weaknesses from a scriptural perspective. Nevertheless, I strongly believe that the Scriptures teach that every infant who dies is immediately ushered into God's glorious presence in heaven. In what follows, I will present the scriptural considerations that have settled the issue in my mind.

The Universal Need of Salvation

At the outset, we must recognize that the whole of Scripture points to the universal need of salvation—even among little children. All of us are born into this world with a sin nature and are in need of redemption. All of us—including infants who cannot believe—are lost (Luke 19:10), perishing (John 3:16), condemned (John 3:18), and are under God's wrath (John 3:36).[2]

How do we know that everyone is born into this world with a

sin nature? In Psalm 51:5 David said, "Surely I was sinful at birth, sinful from the time my mother conceived me." All people, before being redeemed by Christ, are "by nature objects of wrath" (Ephesians 2:3). All descendants of Adam are born in sin (1 Corinthians 15:22). "There is no one righteous, not even one" (Romans 3:10).

Therefore, we cannot say that little children are in a sinless state. We cannot say that children are in an already-redeemed state while they are yet little children. We cannot solve the issue as to whether deceased infants go to heaven by eliminating or lessening their guilt.

As theologian Robert Lightner puts it so well,

> Babies are beautiful and lovely, but they are also lost. They are delightful, but also depraved. They are filled with life, but they are also dead in trespasses and sins. It is not their acts of sin which place them in a state of sin. They are depraved and under divine condemnation at the moment of birth. Apart from Jesus Christ there is no salvation, neither for those who *can* nor for those who *cannot* believe.[3]

When Do Children Become "Responsible"?

Of course, there does come a time when children become morally responsible before God. Christians have often debated what "age" constitutes the so-called *age of accountability*. Actually, it is not the same for every person. Some children mature faster than others. Some come into an awareness of personal evil and righteousness before others do.

One Bible verse that helps us to make sense of this issue is James 4:17: "Anyone, then, who knows the good he ought to do and doesn't do it, sins." It would seem that when a child truly comes into a full awareness and moral understanding of "oughts" and "shoulds," he or she at that point has reached the age of accountability.[4]

Even though the child does not become morally responsible before God until this time, I must emphasize that he or she nevertheless has a sin nature that alienates him or her from God from the moment of birth. *All* human beings are thus engulfed in sin. And whatever solution one comes up with in regard to the issue of infant salvation must deal with this problem.

The solution, it seems to me, must be that at the moment the infant dies—and not before—the benefits of Jesus' atoning death on the cross are applied to him or her. At that moment, the infant becomes saved and is immediately issued into the presence of God in heaven. This view is in keeping not just with the love of God, but with His holiness as well.

God's Purpose in Salvation

In addressing this important issue, it is critical to realize that God's primary purpose in saving human beings is to display His wondrous grace. In Ephesians 1:7-8 we read, "In him we have redemption through his blood, the forgiveness of sins, in accordance with the riches of God's grace that he lavished on us with all wisdom and understanding."

One must ask, "Would the 'riches of God's grace' be displayed in wisdom and understanding in sending babies and little children to hell?" I think not. It would be a cruel mockery for God to call upon infants to do—and to hold them responsible for doing—what they *could not* do. At that young age children simply do not have the capacity to exercise saving faith in Christ.

I believe it is the uniform testimony of Scripture that those who are not capable of making a decision to receive Jesus Christ, and who have died, are now with Christ in heaven, resting in

His tender arms, enjoying the sweetness of His love. There are numerous factors that lend support to this viewpoint, the most important of which I summarize below.

No Infants Mentioned in Hell

It is highly revealing that in all the descriptions of hell in the Bible, we never read of infants or little children there. *Not once.* Only adults capable of making decisions are seen there. Nor do we read of infants and little children standing before the great white throne judgment, which is the judgment of the wicked dead and the precursor to the lake of fire (Revelation 20:11-15).

The complete silence of Scripture regarding the presence of infants in eternal torment militates against their being there. "Not once in all the references to infants is there so much as a hint that they will ever be damned to eternal perdition after death, should they die before they have opportunity to respond to the gospel."[5]

Jesus and Little Children

As we examine instances in which Christ encountered children during His earthly ministry, it would seem that children have a special place in His kingdom. Consider the following moving account of Jesus' interaction with little children:

> At that time the disciples came to Jesus and asked, "Who is the greatest in the kingdom of heaven?"
>
> He called a little child and had him stand among them. And he said: "I tell you the truth, unless you change and become like little children, you will never enter the kingdom of heaven. Therefore, whoever humbles himself like this child is the greatest in the kingdom of heaven.

"And whoever welcomes a little child like this in my name welcomes me. But if anyone causes one of these little ones who believe in me to sin, it would be better for him to have a large millstone hung around his neck and to be drowned in the depths of the sea....

"See that you do not look down on one of these little ones. For I tell you that their angels in heaven always see the face of my Father in heaven.

"What do you think? If a man owns a hundred sheep, and one of them wanders away, will he not leave the ninety-nine on the hills and go to look for the one that wandered off? And if he finds it, I tell you the truth, he is happier about that one sheep than about the ninety-nine that did not wander off. In the same way your Father in heaven is not willing that any of these little ones should be lost" (Matthew 18:1-14).

None of the little children opposed Jesus. All of them allowed Jesus to do with them as He pleased. There was no rejection on their part. And, oh, how Jesus loved them! I do not think there is any way someone could read this passage and conclude that it is within the realm of possibility that Jesus could damn such little ones to hell!

The Attributes of God

The attributes of God certainly relate to the issue of heaven for those who cannot believe.[6] For example, God is characterized by *wisdom*. In His wisdom He chose a plan specifically designed to bring the most glory to Himself. It certainly would not be glorifying to God if little infants and mentally handicapped people who died were condemned to hell because they were incapable of placing saving faith in Christ.

God is characterized by *love*. We read in 1 John 4:16, "We know and rely on the love God has for us. God is love." God not only loves, He *is* love. And it is in keeping with the love of God to incorporate in the plan of salvation a means of saving those who are utterly incapable of believing in Him.[7]

God is characterized by *mercy* and *grace*. "Grace" refers to God's undeserved favor. "Mercy" refers to the withholding of deserved punishment. God not only shows undeserved favor to people but He withholds deserved punishment (see Psalm 103:8-10). How could God be gracious and merciful if He failed to incorporate in the plan of salvation a means of saving those who are utterly incapable of believing in Him?

God is characterized by *goodness*. Nahum 1:7 tells us that "the LORD is good." Psalm 31:19 affirms, "How great is [God's] goodness." Surely God in His goodness would not require of an infant something the infant could not possibly do. God in His goodness would not damn forever someone who could not meet the requirement for salvation which He Himself set forth. God in His goodness would surely incorporate in the plan of salvation a means of saving those who are utterly incapable of believing in Him.

God is also characterized by *justice* (Genesis 18:25; Psalm 11:7; Zephaniah 3:5; John 17:25; Romans 3:26; Hebrews 6:10). Zephaniah 3:5 says, "Morning by morning he dispenses his justice, and every new day he does not fail." Psalm 103:6 affirms, "The LORD works righteousness and justice for all the oppressed." Surely in His justice the Lord would not demand of a creature (like an infant) something that the creature could not do (such as exercising saving faith). As theologian Robert Lightner put it, "How would God be just in refusing into His presence those who were never able to receive or reject His salvation?"[8]

Related to this is the fact that, from a scriptural perspective,

God's wrath comes upon people only because they refuse God's way of escape. Ultimately human beings choose God's wrath themselves. It is poured out only on His enemies—and *those who cannot believe in Him are not His enemies!*

J.I. Packer explains it this way: "God's wrath in the Bible is something which men choose for themselves. Before hell is an experience inflicted by God, it is a state for which man himself opts, by retreating from the light which God shines in his heart to lead him to Himself."[9] Since infants lack this ability to choose, they cannot possibly be the objects of God's wrath. It makes much more sense to say that God in His wisdom, love, mercy, grace, and goodness would incorporate in the plan of salvation a means of saving those who are utterly incapable of believing in Him.

King David and His Son

King David in the Old Testament certainly believed that in the afterlife he would again be with his son who died.[10] In 2 Samuel 12:22-23 David said, "While the child was still alive, I fasted and wept. I thought, 'Who knows? The LORD may be gracious to me and let the child live.' But now that he is dead, why should I fast? Can I bring him back again? *I will go to him,* but he will not return to me" (emphasis added). David displayed complete confidence that his little one was with God in heaven, and that he would one day join his son in heaven.[11] As one theologian put it,

> Life after death was a certainty for David. That he would in the future again be with his son was his firm belief...David was rightly related to Jehovah, and he had no doubt that he would spend eternity with Him. Neither did he have any doubt that his infant son, taken in death before he could decide for or against his father's God, would be there also.[12]

The Basis of the Judgment of the Lost

Another consideration that points to the assurance of infant salvation relates to the basis of the judgment of the lost. We read in Revelation 20:11-13:

> Then I saw a great white throne and him who was seated on it. Earth and sky fled from his presence, and there was no place for them. And I saw the dead, great and small, standing before the throne, and books were opened. Another book was opened, which is the book of life. The dead were judged *according to what they had done* as recorded in the books. The sea gave up the dead that were in it, and death and Hades gave up the dead that were in them, and each person was judged *according to what he had done* (emphasis added).

The basis of this judgment of the wicked is clearly deeds done while on earth (see also Psalm 62:12; Proverbs 24:12; Matthew 16:27; Romans 2:6; 2 Corinthians 5:10; Revelation 2:23). Hence, infants and mentally handicapped people cannot possibly be the objects of this judgment because they are not responsible for their deeds. Such a judgment against infants would be a travesty. As J. Sidlow Baxter puts it, "It is unthinkable that such infants should be judged and condemned…There is nothing they have done on which judgment could be passed, and therefore nothing for which to be condemned."[13] Kenneth Boa and Robert Bowman likewise write: "Unborn children, infants, and the mentally incapable are incapable of doing either good or evil (Deuteronomy 1:39; Isaiah 7:15-16; Romans 9:11) and therefore cannot do anything deserving of condemnation…. Therefore, no unborn children, infant, or mentally incapable people will be condemned."[14]

Dying Infants and the Mentally Challenged
Must Therefore Be Among "The Elect"

If infants will not be condemned, how does the issue of infant salvation relate to the doctrine of election? Election is that sovereign act of God of choosing certain individuals to salvation before the foundation of the world. It is my belief, with many other Christians, that God's election is based on His sovereign choice. A number of biblical arguments support this view:

- Biblical statements support election by sovereign choice (Acts 13:48).

- The whole process of salvation is a gift of God (Romans 12:3; Ephesians 2:8-10).

- Certain verses speak of human beings having been given to Christ by the Father (John 6:37; 17:2), and of the Father drawing men to Christ (John 6:44).

- There are examples in Scripture of the sovereign calling of God upon individuals, such as Paul (Galatians 1:15) and Jeremiah (Jeremiah 1:5), even before they were born.

- Election is compatible with God's sovereignty (Jeremiah 10:23; Proverbs 19:21).

- Election is portrayed as being from all eternity (2 Timothy 1:9).

In view of such scriptural factors, it is my belief that all infants (as well as mentally challenged people) who die do indeed go to heaven, and are therefore to be numbered among the elect of God. In keeping with this, J. Oswald Sanders cites the Confession of Faith of the Christian Reformed Church: "We believe that all dying in infancy are included in the election of grace and are regenerated and saved by Christ through the Spirit who works when and how he pleases."[15] I am convinced that this view is correct.

What About Miscarried Babies?

If this view is correct, then what about aborted or miscarried babies? Do they have eternal souls while they are yet in the womb? And do they go to heaven at the moment of death?

I believe the answer to both questions must be *yes*. The Scriptures indicate that at the very moment of conception the babe in the womb possesses a soul. Many Christians, myself included, believe that children receive from their parents—through conception—*both* their material part (the body) *and* immaterial part (the soul or spirit). According to this view, Adam begat a son *in his own likeness*, and this would have to include Adam's *entire* likeness—both body and soul (Genesis 5:3). After all, Scripture indicates that *all* living beings reproduce *after their kind* (see Genesis 1:3,6,9,11,14,20,24), and "human beings" are comprised of both body and soul (or spirit). So, reproduction must include both body and soul.

Since babies in the womb have eternal souls, then all the arguments in this chapter regarding infant salvation must therefore apply to preborn infants as well. The moment a baby in the womb is aborted, his or her soul or spirit departs from the body and goes directly to heaven. The moment a baby in the womb is miscarried, his or her soul departs from the body and goes directly to heaven.

If it is true that all children who die in the womb or in infancy will be saved, along with all those with mental incapacities, the implications for the population of heaven is staggering. Considering the rates for miscarriages, stillborn deaths, and infant mortality for most of human history (and even today), the number of such children whom we may expect to live forever in God's kingdom will conservatively be in the billions. They might even end up outnumbering the responsible older children and adults who are saved through their faith.

Heaven for Those Who Can't Believe

What, then, can we conclude in view of all the above? The scriptural position on infant salvation may be summarized as follows:

- Every infant born into the world is born with a sin nature that causes him or her to be alienated from God.

- Every child eventually comes into moral awareness at the age of accountability.

- If a child should die before reaching the age of accountability, the benefits of Christ's death are applied to that child at the moment of death (and not before), and the child is issued immediately into the presence of God in heaven.

- This view is consistent with the fact that the purpose of God in saving human beings is to show forth His grace and mercy.

- This view is consistent with all the attributes of God— including His love, goodness, and justice.

- This view is consistent with what Jesus said about children in the New Testament.

- This view is consistent with the fact that only adults are portrayed as being judged (and held volitionally responsible for their evil deeds) at the great white throne judgment and then cast into the lake of fire.

We may rest with certainty, then, that children who die before coming into moral awareness—which, I firmly believe, includes preborn babies—are resting happily and serenely in the tender arms of Jesus. They are resting securely in the sweetness of His infinite love. They are the special objects of His tender affection and care. In the words of one of the most widely sung hymns of all time,

> Jesus loves the little children,
>> All the children of the world;
> Red and yellow, black and white,
>> All are precious in His sight:
> Jesus loves the little children of the world.
>> Jesus died for all the children,
> All the children of the world;
>> Red and yellow, black and white,
> All are precious in His sight:
>> Jesus died for all the children of
>> the world.

11

REWARDS FOR
FAITHFUL SERVICE

O ur wonderful God is a God who rewards. Scripture is virtually brimming with examples of how faithful living on earth will yield future rewards in heaven.[1] We see this throughout both the Old and New Testaments. Following are just a few scriptural highlights:

- "Surely the righteous still are rewarded; surely there is a God who judges the earth" (Psalm 58:11).

- "You, O Lord, are loving. Surely you will reward each person according to what he has done" (Psalm 62:12).

- "He who sows righteousness reaps a sure reward" (Proverbs 11:18).

- "The Sovereign LORD comes with power...See, his reward is with him, and his recompense accompanies him" (Isaiah 40:10).

- "See, your Savior comes! See, his reward is with him, and his recompense accompanies him" (Isaiah 62:11).

- "Rejoice and be glad, because great is your reward in heaven, for in the same way they persecuted the prophets who were before you" (Matthew 5:12).

- "Be careful not to do your 'acts of righteousness' before men, to be seen by them. If you do, you will have no reward from your Father in heaven. So when you give to the needy, do not announce it with trumpets, as the hypocrites do in the synagogues and on the streets, to be honored by men. I tell you the truth, they have received their reward in full" (Matthew 6:1-2).

- "Anyone who receives a prophet because he is a prophet will receive a prophet's reward, and anyone who receives a righteous man because he is a righteous man will receive a righteous man's reward. And if anyone gives even a cup of cold water to one of these little ones because he is my disciple, I tell you the truth, he will certainly not lose his reward" (Matthew 10:41-42).

- "Love your enemies, do good to them, and lend to them without expecting to get anything back. Then your reward will be great, and you will be sons of the Most High..." (Luke 6:35).

- "The man who plants and the man who waters have one purpose, and each will be rewarded according to his own labor" (1 Corinthians 3:8).

- "If what he has built survives [using good instead of worthless materials in 'building' his life], he will receive his reward" (1 Corinthians 3:14, insert added for clarification).

- "You know that the Lord will reward everyone for whatever good he does, whether he is slave or free" (Ephesians 6:8).

- "Do not throw away your confidence; it will be richly rewarded. You need to persevere so that when you have done the will of God, you will receive what he has promised" (Hebrews 10:35-36).

- "Without faith it is impossible to please God, because anyone who comes to him must believe that he exists and that he rewards those who earnestly seek him" (Hebrews 11:6).

- "By faith Moses, when he had grown up, refused to be known as the son of Pharaoh's daughter. He chose to be mistreated along with the people of God rather than to enjoy the pleasures of sin for a short time. He regarded disgrace for the sake of Christ as of greater value than the treasures of Egypt, because he was looking ahead to his reward" (Hebrews 11:24-26).

- "Watch out that you do not lose what you have worked for, but that you may be rewarded fully" (2 John 1:8).

- "The time has come...for rewarding your servants the prophets and your saints and those who reverence your name, both small and great..." (Revelation 11:18).

- "Behold, I am coming soon! My reward is with me,

and I will give to everyone according to what he has
done" (Revelation 22:12).

So, I say again, our God is a God who rewards. This is both a
wonderful and a *sobering* teaching of Scripture. After all, when
our life on this earth is over and we face Christ the divine Judge,
we will either *receive* or possibly *forfeit* rewards. This teaching is
thus *wonderful* in the sense that it can motivate us to live faithfully for Christ during our short sojourn on earth. It is *sobering*
because if we choose unfaithfulness, we may surely forfeit what
could have been ours.

For this reason, John Wesley, in one of his famous sermons,
commented, "Every man shall give an account of his own works,
a full and true account of all that he ever did while alive, whether
it was good or evil."[2] Such words are needed in times like these. It
seems that few people today—*Christians included*—govern their
actions with a view to being held accountable for them at a future
judgment.[3] Though many prefer to ignore any mention of the
subject, the fact remains that the possibility of receiving and/or
losing rewards in the afterlife can be a powerful motivator regarding how we live our lives!

The Judgment Seat of Christ

All Christians will one day stand before "God's judgment seat"
(Romans 14:8-10), also known as the "judgment seat of Christ"
(2 Corinthians 5:10). At that time each believer's life will be exam-
ined in regard to deeds done while in the body. Personal motives
and intents of the heart will also be weighed. J. Oswald Sanders
observes that "all true believers who stand before the judgment
seat will qualify for heaven, but not all will receive the same
reward."[4] His point is that all true believers are saved and are in
no danger of losing their salvation, but some believers—because

of their faithful service to God—will receive more rewards than other lesser-committed Christians. In keeping with this, the great Puritan preacher Jonathan Edwards was convinced that "heaven, like everywhere else, would be hierarchical; some would be above others in glory, but such differences would cause no diminishment of happiness because all would wish only fullest happiness for others."[5]

The idea of a "judgment seat" relates to the athletic games of Paul's day. As Pastor Douglas Connelly puts it, "After the races and games concluded, a dignitary or even the emperor himself took his seat on an elevated throne in the arena. One by one the winning athletes came up to the throne to receive a reward—usually a wreath of leaves, a victor's crown."[6] In the case of Christians, each of us will stand before Christ the Judge and receive (or possibly forfeit) rewards.

Christ's judgment of us will not be in a corporate setting—like a big class being praised or scolded by a teacher. Rather it will be individual and personal. "We will all stand before God's judgment seat" (Romans 14:10). Each of us will be judged on an individual basis. Scripture indicates that "God's evaluation of the believer's life will be based upon all that has been given to him or her in the way of time, treasures, talents, and truth."[7]

Moreover, at the judgment seat of Christ all earthly inequities will be righted once and for all—including inequities committed among Christians. Can you think of a time when you witnessed a believer suffering wrongfully at the hands of a fellow believer? Can you think of a time when a humble Christian suffered cruelty at the hands of a proud and carnal believer? Such injustices as these will be vindicated on that day of judgment. The Lord "will bring to light what is hidden in darkness and will expose the motives of men's hearts" (1 Corinthians 4:5).

I must again emphasize that this judgment has nothing to

do with whether or not the Christian will remain saved. Those who have placed faith in Christ *are* saved, and nothing threatens that. Believers are eternally secure in their salvation (John 10:28-30; Romans 8:28-30; Ephesians 1:13; 4:30; Hebrews 7:25). According to one theologian, "It should be clear from the general doctrine of justification by faith* and the fact that the believer is the object of the grace of God that this is not an occasion in which the believers are punished for their sins. All who are in Christ Jesus are declared to have 'no condemnation' (Romans 8:1)."[8] This judgment rather has to do only with the reception or loss of rewards.

Scripture indicates that this judgment will take place immediately after the church is "raptured"** and Christ takes the saints back to heaven. No Bible verse explicitly states this, but a number of factors lead us to this conclusion.

For one thing, many scholars believe that the 24 elders in heaven that are mentioned in Revelation 4:10 represent believers—and they are portrayed as *already having* their crowns in heaven at the very start of the Tribulation period. Moreover, when the bride of Christ (the corporate body of Christians) returns to earth with Christ at the second coming, the bride is clothed with "righteous acts"—implying that she has already passed through the judgment (Revelation 19:8).

---

* We become "justified" the moment we trust in Christ. Biblical justification is a singular and instantaneous event in which God judicially (legally) declares the believing sinner to be absolutely righteous and not guilty (Romans 3:25,28,30; 8:33-34; Galatians 4:21–5:12; 1 John 1:7–2:2). This legal declaration is something external to a person. It does not hinge on a person's individual level of righteousness. It does not hinge on anything that a person does. It hinges solely on God's declaration. It is a once-and-for-all judicial pronouncement that takes place the moment a sinner places faith in Christ. Even while a person is yet a sinner and is experientially not righteous, he or she is nevertheless righteous in God's sight because of forensic justification (Romans 3:25,28,30).

**The "Rapture" is that future event—just prior to the beginning of the Tribulation period—in which Christ will remove all the Christians from the world and take them back to heaven (1 Corinthians 15:51-52; 1 Thessalonians 4:13-17). At the Rapture, believers will receive their glorified resurrection bodies.

The sobering part of all this is the scriptural indication that some believers at the judgment may have a sense of deprivation and suffer some degree of forfeiture and shame. Indeed, certain rewards may be forfeited that otherwise might have been received, and this will involve a sense of loss. The reality is, Christians differ radically in holiness of conduct and faithfulness in service. God in His justice and holiness takes all this into account. Some believers will be without shame and others with shame at the judgment seat of Christ.

This is the reason 2 John 8 urges, "Watch out that you do not lose what you have worked for, but that you may be rewarded fully." In 1 John 2:28 John had earlier written about the possibility of a believer actually being ashamed at Christ's coming.

We must keep all this in perspective, however. Christ's coming for us at the Rapture, and the prospect of living eternally with Him, is something that should give each of us joy. And our joy will last for all eternity. How, then, can we reconcile this eternal joy with the possible forfeiture of reward and perhaps even some level of shame at the judgment seat of Christ?

I think Herman Hoyt's explanation is the best I have seen:

> The Judgment Seat of Christ might be compared to a commencement ceremony. At graduation there is some measure of disappointment and remorse that one did not do better and work harder. However, at such an event the overwhelming emotion is joy, not remorse. The graduates do not leave the auditorium weeping because they did not earn better grades. Rather, they are thankful that they have been graduated, and they are grateful for what they did achieve. To *overdo* the sorrow aspect of the Judgment Seat of Christ is to make heaven hell. To *underdo* the sorrow aspect is to make faithfulness inconsequential.[9]

Let Us Therefore Build Christ-Honoring Lives

In 1 Corinthians 3:11-15 the apostle Paul tells us:

> No one can lay any foundation other than the one already laid, which is Jesus Christ. If any man builds on this foundation using gold, silver, costly stones, wood, hay or straw, his work will be shown for what it is, because the Day will bring it to light. It will be revealed with fire, and the fire will test the quality of each man's work. If what he has built survives, he will receive his reward. If it is burned up, he will suffer loss; he himself will be saved, but only as one escaping through the flames.

Theologian John Walvoord suggested that every Christian actually has the foundation of Jesus Christ, since they are saved. However, some build a life of effective service on that foundation, while others build a shaky structure of feeble spiritual commitment on that foundation: "In using the figure of a building, attention is called first of all to the fact that it must be built on the proper foundation, namely, salvation in Christ. Everyone who appears at the judgment seat of Christ will meet this qualification as a person who has put his trust in Christ and has been accepted in the Beloved. Upon the foundation of our salvation in Christ, it is necessary for us to erect our lives."[10] It is up to each of us individually as to what kind of materials we will use to erect our lives—*worthy* or *unworthy*. Walvoord urged that "our lives should be lived in such a way that they will have eternal value, and the time and effort extended will be worthy of reward by the Lord at the judgment seat of Christ."[11]

Notice that the materials Paul mentioned in this passage are combustible in increasing degrees. Obviously the hay and straw are the most combustible. Then comes wood. Precious metals and stones are not combustible.

It also seems clear that some of these materials are useful for building while others are not. If you construct a house made of hay or straw, it surely will not stand for very long. (And it can burn to the ground very easily.) But a house constructed with solid materials such as stones and metals will stand and last a long time.

What do these building materials represent? One Christian leader insightfully suggested that "gold, silver, and costly stones refer to the fruit of the Spirit in our lives; they refer to Christ-honoring motives and godly obedience and transparent integrity. Wood, hay, and straw are perishable things—carnal attitudes, sinful motives, pride-filled actions, selfish ambition."[12]

In Scripture, fire often symbolizes the holiness of God (Hebrews 12:29). God, then, will examine our works, and they will be tested against the fire of His holiness. If our works are built with good materials—like precious metals and stones—our works will stand. But if our works are built with less valuable materials—wood, hay, or straw—they will burn up.

Perhaps the figure is intended to communicate that those works performed with a view to glorifying God are the works that will stand. Those works performed with a view to glorifying self, performed in the flesh, are those that will be burned up.

Apparently some believers will suffer such loss at the judgment seat of Christ that practically all—if not all—of their works go up in flames. Paul describes this person as being saved, "but only as one escaping through the flames" (1 Corinthians 3:15). Theologian Merrill F. Unger explains it this way:

> Imagine yourself waking out of sleep to find your house ablaze. You have no time to save a thing. You

flee with only the night clothes on your back. Even
these are singed away by the flames that engulf you.
You escape with literally nothing but your life…In this
fashion believers who have lived carnally and care-
lessly or who have worked for self and self-interest
instead of for the Lord will find that all their works
have been burned up. They shall have no reward. No
trophies to lay at Jesus' feet! No crowns to rejoice in
that day of judgment![13]

While 1 Corinthians 3:11-15 may seem alarming, my sense of
it is that it is the perpetually *carnal* and *backslidden* Christian who
is in danger of suffering such a total loss of rewards. Generally,
Christians who are committed enough to read Christian books in
order to understand more about God and His Word (like you at
the present moment) are generally not the kind of Christians who
will suffer such total loss. So, sit back and take a deep breath.

I urge you to consider these words in 1 Corinthians 3:11-15 as
more of a *challenge* than a *threat*. More specifically, consider it a
challenge to joyfully live for Jesus, seek to obey Him, and hold on
to those rewards. Don't go about daily living with the constant,
oppressive mentality that God is like a cosmic Scrooge who is carefully eyeballing your every move with a view to "getting even" at the
judgment. Never forget that God absolutely loves you and passionately *wants* to reward you. He does not want to be put in a position
of having to withhold rewards. *God is on your side!* Since that is true,
let's reciprocate by showing our love for Him by living the way He
wants us to. If we do that, there *will* be rewards to be received.

Run the Race Well

Later, in 1 Corinthians 9:24-27, the apostle Paul further
instructed:

Do you not know that in a race all the runners run, but only one gets the prize? Run in such a way as to get the prize. Everyone who competes in the games goes into strict training. They do it to get a crown that will not last; but we do it to get a crown that will last forever. Therefore I do not run like a man running aimlessly; I do not fight like a man beating the air. No, I beat my body and make it my slave so that after I have preached to others, I myself will not be disqualified for the prize.

The reference to being disqualified in this verse refers not to *salvation* but to *rewards*. "It is a picture of an athlete who by breaking the rules is disqualified from winning the race. The figure makes plain that a Christian should bend all his efforts to living in such a way that he will not be ashamed when his life is reviewed at the judgment seat of Christ."[14] So, like Paul, we should make every effort to avoid being disqualified.

Understanding the athletic events of Paul's day helps us to better grasp Paul's point. Among the Greeks one of the most thrilling sporting events was the Isthmian games that were celebrated every two years in the city of Corinth. Two of the games at this event were foot racing and boxing.

In foot racing, one must obviously engage in a sustained effort to win the prize. Applying this to spiritual things, Paul urged Christians to "run in such a way that you may win." In other words, the Christian should seek to live a *sustained* life of faithfulness. Just as an athlete must continually apply self-discipline and be self-controlled in all areas in order to win the race, so also must the Christian apply self-discipline and be self-controlled with the ultimate goal of pleasing the Lord at the judgment seat of Christ.[15]

Allow me to encourage you to not give up. Don't throw in the towel in frustration. If you should stumble and fall, pick your-self up again and get back into the race. Do you remember the famous Eric Liddell—the "flying Scotsman"—as portrayed in the blockbuster movie, *Chariots of Fire*? When he fell during a race, he picked himself up and got right back in the race. That's what we should do! We all stumble from time to time (James 3:2), but let's commit to being distance runners all the way to heaven!

In boxing, one must be self-controlled and be well trained in order to render well-landed blows to the opponent. Applying this to spiritual things, Paul said he directed well-aimed blows at his own body in order to keep it under subjection. One must guard against carnal desires. Guarding against such desires helps one to keep in good spiritual shape.

Those who won the Greek games received a mere "perishable wreath"—a wreath made of wild olive and parsley that fades over time. This contrasts with the "imperishable" awards that will be handed out to faithful Christians at Christ's judgment seat (more on this shortly).

The Scope of the Judgment Includes Actions

The Christian's judgment will focus on his personal stew-ardship of the gifts, talents, opportunities, and responsibilities given to him in this life. The very character of each Christian's life and service will be utterly laid bare under the unerring and omniscient vision of Christ, whose eyes are "as a flame of fire" (Revelation 1:14 NASB).

Numerous Scripture verses reveal that each of our actions will be judged before the Lord. The psalmist said to the Lord, "Surely you will reward each person according to what he has done" (Psalm 62:12; see also Matthew 16:27). In Ephesians 6:8, we read that the Lord "will reward everyone for whatever good he does, whether he is slave or free."

Christ's judgment of our actions will be infallible. There will be no confusion on His part. His understanding of the circumstances under which we committed acts on earth will be fully understood by Him. As John Wesley once put it, "God will then bring to light every circumstance that accompanied each word and action. He will judge whether they lessened or increased the goodness or badness of them."[16]

This is obviously both a warning and a comfort. It is a warning because we will not get away with any wrongdoing we have committed. It is a comfort because Christ, with His all-seeing eye, will be aware of all the small unnoticed (and therefore unappreciated) kindnesses you rendered to others throughout your life on earth. *Jesus is a perfect Judge.*

The Scope of the Judgment Includes Thoughts

At the judgment seat of Christ, it won't just be our actions that will come under scrutiny. Also scrutinized will be our thoughts. In Jeremiah 17:10 God said, "I the LORD search the heart and examine the mind, to reward a man according to his conduct, according to what his deeds deserve." The Lord "will bring to light what is hidden in darkness and will expose the motives of men's hearts" (1 Corinthians 4:5). The Lord is the One "who searches hearts and minds" (Revelation 2:23).

Again, this is both a warning and a comfort. It is a warning because all selfish motives will be uncovered. It is a comfort because the Lord will also uncover those good motives of certain actions you engaged in that may have been misinterpreted or misunderstood by other people. *Jesus is a perfect Judge.*

The Scope of the Judgment Includes Words

Finally, the scope of the believer's judgment will include all the words he or she has spoken. Christ once said that "men will have to give account on the day of judgment for every careless word they have spoken" (Matthew 12:36). This is an important aspect of judgment, for tremendous damage can be done through the tongue (see James 3:1-12).

John Blanchard reminds us that "if even our careless words are carefully recorded, how can we bear the thought that our calculated boastful claims, the cutting criticisms, the off-color jokes, and the unkind comments—will also be taken into account. Even our whispered asides and words spoken in confidence or when we thought we were 'safe' will be heard again."[17] The balance, though, is that Christ will also be fully aware of how you used your tongue to bless others—such as the encouraging words you spoke to your child, the compliment you gave your pastor, your comforting words to a grieving widow, or the time you shared the gospel with your neighbor. *Jesus is a perfect Judge.*

A Comprehensive Judgment

From the above, it seems more than clear that our judgment will be a *comprehensive* judgment. This becomes all the clearer as we peruse the rest of Scripture. Indeed, Scripture reveals that we will be held accountable for how we use our God-given talents and abilities (Matthew 25:14-29; Luke 19:11-26; 2 Timothy 1:6-7; 1 Peter 4:10) and how we spent our time (Psalm 90:9-12; Ephesians 5:16; Colossians 4:5; 1 Peter 1:17). We will be held accountable for how we treat others (Hebrews 6:10; Matthew 10:41-42), our hospitality to strangers (Matthew 25:35-36; Luke 14:12-14), responding in a godly way to mistreatment (Matthew 5:11-12; Mark 10:29-30; Luke 6:27-28,35; Romans 8:18; 2 Corinthians 4:17; 1 Peter 4:12-13), and making efforts toward winning souls for Christ (Proverbs 11:30; Daniel 12:3; 1 Thessalonians 2:19-20). We will also be held accountable for our attitude toward money (Matthew 6:1-4; 1 Timothy 6:17-19).[18]

If you are like most people, your eyes might tend to become as wide as pancakes when contemplating such a list. But let us not forget that 100 percent of all of us have *regularly failed in all these areas.* (Praise Jesus that He took upon Himself all our sins, and all our failures, at the cross—2 Corinthians 5:21.) The balance is that God is also fully aware of that dinner you cooked for a sick friend. He is fully aware of the time you spoke kind words to that person at work who seemed to be having a bad day. He is fully aware of the many people you have prayed for throughout your life. He is fully aware of the efforts you have made (feeble though they may be) in sharing the gospel with others. He is aware of all the nice things you have done that most human beings were completely oblivious to.

My point is that even though we will all fall short in many areas when we face the Lord at the judgment (I'm sure I will), we can rest assured that Christ's sacrifice has covered all our sins (including all our sinful actions, thoughts, and words), and that the Lord will reward each of us for the things that He deems good, compassionate, worthy, and righteous. Never forget that He is a perfect Judge. And never forget that He loves you passionately.

Rewards and Crowns

What kinds of rewards will believers receive at the judgment seat of Christ? Scripture often speaks of them in terms of crowns that we wear. Christian scholar Arnold Fruchtenbaum tells us that the Greek language has two words for "crown":

> One is the word *diadem,* which is a king's crown. It is the crown of a sovereign and of a person who is royal by his nature and by his position—a king. This is the kind of crown that Jesus wears. The second Greek

word is *stephanos,* which is a crown given to an over-
comer, a victor, one who has won a race.[19]

There are a number of different crowns that symbolize the
various spheres of achievement and award in the Christian life:

- The *crown of life* is given to those who persevere under
  trial, and especially to those who suffer to the point of
  death (James 1:12; Revelation 2:10).

- The *crown of glory* is given to those who faithfully and
  sacrificially minister God's Word to the flock (1 Peter
  5:4). It is available to pastors, elders, and others who
  feed God's sheep with the milk and meat of the Word
  of God.[20]

- The *crown incorruptible* is given to those who win the
  race of temperance and self-control (1 Corinthians
  9:24-25). "It is for those who have gained the victory
  over the old man, the old sin nature. It is for those who
  have learned to live a Spirit-controlled life."[21]

- The *crown of righteousness* is given to those who long
  for the second coming of Christ (2 Timothy 4:7-8).
  Arnold Fruchtenbaum suggests that "this is a crown
  for those who have kept the faith both doctrinally and
  morally in spite of adverse circumstances. It is a crown
  given to those who love his appearing, those who look
  longingly for the return of the Messiah. Looking for
  His return is the result of sound doctrine and keeping
  the faith."[22]

- The *crown of rejoicing* is given to believers who win
  souls to Christ. "It is a crown available to all those
  who do the work of evangelism, and the fruits of their

labors are seen in people coming to the Lord through them."[23]

Though these are the only specific rewards mentioned in the Bible, I am sure the Lord has many other perfect rewards, each suitable and appropriate for various spheres of achievement.

It is highly revealing that in Revelation 4:10 we find believers casting their crowns before the throne of God in an act of worship and adoration. This teaches us something very important. Clearly the crowns (as rewards) are bestowed on us not for our own glory but ultimately for the glory of God. We are told elsewhere in Scripture that believers are redeemed in order to bring glory to God (1 Corinthians 6:20). It would seem that the act of placing our crowns before the throne of God is an illustration of this.

Here is something else to think about: The greater reward or crown one has received, the greater capacity one has to bring glory to the Creator. The lesser reward or crown one has received, the lesser is his capacity to bring glory to the Creator. Because of the different rewards handed out at the judgment seat of Christ, believers will have differing capacities to bring glory to God. According to Pastor Mark Hitchcock, "Some of us will be twenty-watt bulbs, some sixty, some seventy-five, and someone one hundred. We will all shine, but some more than others."[24]

In view of this clear teaching from Scripture, theologian Norman Geisler suggests: "Everyone in heaven will be *fully* blessed, but not everyone will be *equally* blessed. Every believers' cup will be full and running over, but not everyone's cup will be the same size. We determine *in time* what our capacity for appreciating God will be *in eternity*."[25]

Still, we shouldn't take this to mean that certain believers will have a sense of loss throughout eternity. After all, each believer will be glorifying God to the fullness of his capacity in the next life. Each one of us, then, will be able to "declare the praises of him who called [us] out of darkness into his wonderful light" (1 Peter 2:9).[26]

So, *be encouraged.* Your God loves you and delights in your spiritual successes, yearning to reward you one day. Let us therefore resolve to serve Him with joy and full conviction that He always seeks our highest good—both here on earth and in our future in heaven.

12

HELPING THOSE
WHO GRIEVE

While this is a book about heaven, the reality is that before *we* get to heaven, we have to suffer the loss of Christian loved ones and friends dying and going to heaven *before us*. To be sure, we rejoice over the fact that they are in heaven and are with the Lord Jesus Christ, but we nevertheless feel the pain of grief.

There is no pain like the pain of grief. Some would say it is the most oppressive and suffocating pain a human being can endure. It often seems to come in relentless waves, providing little chance for rest or relief.

While doing research for this book, I came across a deeply moving, heart-wrenching account of a man in deep grief. His story powerfully reflects what each of us can go through when a loved one dies:

The rays of a late morning South Carolina sun struck me full on the face as I stepped through the door of the hospital. The squint of my eyes, however, was not occasioned by the rays of the sun; it was the visible display of the anguish and despair that wracked my very life.

I had spent several hours with my sobbing wife. Now I was about to keep the appointment that would prove to be the emotional climax of the day my world collapsed.

On my way to the appointment, I stopped at a diner to have a cup of coffee and to bolster my courage. I was oblivious to everything except the appointment that awaited me.

Leaving the diner, I made my way to a large white house, located on a corner in Columbia, South Carolina. I followed the owner into a large room, where he soon left me alone. I slowly made my way across a thick rug on the floor to a table on the far side of the room.

Upon the table was a white box. I stood before that white box for endless eternities before I finally summoned enough courage to look over the top and down into the white box, at the lifeless body of my son.

At that sight my world collapsed. I would have given up all of my academic and athletic awards. I would have given up the prestigious executive training program I was engaged in with one of the largest international oil companies. I would have given anything. For the first time in my life, I had come to a hurdle I could not clear. My world collapsed.[1]

Death hurts. It hurts deeply—*even* for Christians who have a strong faith in God, resurrection, and the afterlife.

Christians Are Not Immune to Grief

Christians are not immune to the pain of grief. Even though Christ has taken the "sting" out of death (1 Corinthians 15:55), it is nevertheless extremely painful when a family member or friend dies. Even the great apostle Paul considered death an "enemy" yet to be conquered (verse 26).

In Western society many young boys are told from early childhood, "Big boys don't cry." As they reach their teenage years, they are told, "Men don't cry." Upon life's misfortunes they are told, "Take it like a man." Such unfortunate comments fail to recognize that weeping is the language of the soul—and that weeping is the proper response to grief.

Some Christians have wrongly surmised that a "true" Christian who has faith in God should not grieve over the loss of a loved one or friend. But this is a gross distortion of what the Scriptures teach. We must recognize that Scripture clearly distinguishes between those who "grieve" (as believers) and those who "grieve like the rest of men, who have no hope" (1 Thessalonians 4:13).

Do you remember the story of Lazarus's death in Bethany? Lazarus was a close friend of Jesus. And after Lazarus died, Jesus went to Bethany to be with Lazarus's family. We read in John 11:35 that upon witnessing the scene in Bethany, "Jesus wept." Jesus was so deeply moved that He cried over His friend's passing. The Jews that witnessed this said, "See how he loved him!" (verse 36).

It is natural and right for us to be sad, to ache, to grieve and cry when a loved one or friend dies. When Stephen was put to death, we are told "Godly men buried [him] and mourned deeply for him" (Acts 8:2). The apostle Paul acknowledged that if Epaphroditus had died, he himself would have had "sorrow upon sorrow" (Philippians 2:27). Godly Christians can mourn deeply. Again, however, the grief Christians experience over the loss of Christian loved ones or friends is not the same as the grief unbelievers experience. As one Christian leader put it, "Christians do grieve over the loss of loved ones; this is a normal human experience which even Jesus shared (John 11:35). But the grief of Christians differs from that of unbelievers, for the latter have *no hope* of bodily resurrection to glory with Christ (1 Thes. 4:16)."[2]

I recently read of a Christian man, Lyman Coleman, who wrote a letter about the death of his beloved wife, Margaret. He reflected, "The most painful decision of my life was asking God to take her home. She had been suffering from repeated brain seizures and her body was wasted. I whispered in her ear: 'Honey, I love you. I love you. Jesus wants you to come home. We are going to be all right. We give you permission to let go.' She closed her eyes and fell asleep."

In his letter, Lyman went on to say,

> As I write this letter, I realize I am without my editor. My greatest critic. My teammate. Soulmate. Prayer-mate. Partner in everything. We traveled the roads less traveled together in hard times and good times. Honey, I miss you. I miss you. I miss you. I will keep the light on for the kids. I will be there for friends. And one day, we are going to join you. All of us. Because Jesus promised it. "Precious in the sight of the Lord is the death of his saints."[3]

Lyman was *full of grief*. But as a Christian, he was also *full of hope*. He had confidence of a future resurrection and reunion in heaven. *That* is what separates the grief of Christians from the grief of unbelievers. In one case there is hope; in the other, all hope is gone.

Understanding Bereavement

Christians who have the hope of eternal life can be confident that they will spend eternity with their Christian loved ones. That is an incredible source of strength and comfort. Even so, this comforting hope does not eliminate the pain and grief of the present moment.

When Pastor Rick Taylor's young son Kyle died, there came a time when he spoke the following touching words from his heart:

> Kyle is dead. He is gone. I will never see my precious son grow up. I will never throw the football with him again. I will never again help him learn how to grip a bat or clap for joy because he hit a ball. I will never again sit by his side and read to him at bedtime. I will never again go for walks with him…I will never see the man he would have become.[4]

The same kinds of deeply hurtful feelings are present when a spouse dies. Again, it is Pastor Taylor who gives us insight:

> The day-to-day reality faced by the widow is that she will never again be held by her husband in this life. They will never again hold hands as they take strolls under autumn skies. They will never again joke and laugh or hurt and cry together. They will never again watch the sunset together. They will never again lie beside each other in bed and talk together and love together.[5]

This is the pain of bereavement. It is a pain rooted in the harsh reality that in this world we will *never again* do the most precious and dear things with the one who has died. *It is a hurt that wounds the heart like no other hurt.*

Understanding Feelings of Isolation

Christian counselors tell us that the bereaved often feel isolated and cut off from other people—especially in the weeks following the funeral of their loved one. At the funeral there is typically a great outpouring of love. And that is as it should be. But then friends and relatives plow back into their lives, often forgetting the pain that the bereaved continue to experience in the weeks and months that follow. You and I should take this to heart and resolve to remain sensitive to our friends and acquaintances who grieve, and make every effort to stay in regular contact with them during these difficult months.

We should be especially sensitive to the fact that the bereaved often experience feelings of awkwardness, unconnectedness, and even feelings of being stigmatized after the loss of their loved one. Following the death of his wife, C.S. Lewis kept of diary of his daily grief and published it in a book entitled *A Grief Observed*. In it he spoke of the sense of awkwardness he felt in the presence of other people with whom he came into contact following his wife's death:

> An odd byproduct of my loss is that I'm aware of being an embarrassment to everyone I meet. At work, at the club, in the street, I see people, as they approach me, trying to make up their minds whether they'll "say something about it" or not. I hate it if they do, *and* if they don't...R. has been avoiding me for a week. I like best the well-brought-up young men, almost boys, who walk up to me as if I were a dentist, turn very red,

get it over, and then edge away to the bar as quickly as they decently can. Perhaps the bereaved ought to be isolated in special settlements like lepers.[6]

Lewis's words are rightfully a rebuke, and represent a call for us to genuinely *be there* for those who grieve. First and foremost, we can "be there" for our grieving friend or family member by regularly lifting them up in prayer before God. Pray for their emotional stability, their physical health, their spiritual life, their eternal perspective, and ask God for His guidance in how to be of genuine help.

"Being there" also includes recognizing that everyone faces death in their own way, and not necessarily as we would, or think they should. We must be sensitive to discern when our company and spoken support are needed, or when our quiet presence and a listening ear would be more appreciated. The bottom line of "being there" is to be sensitive, thoughtful, and understanding.

Grief Must Be Expressed

Grief *must* be expressed in some way. It is much like the steam in a steam engine. Unless it can escape in a controlled way, the pressure will steadily build up and the boiler will explode. Unless we learn to express grief, we can look forward to an emotional and psychological explosion of some sort. Emotional release is a must.

When we are helping someone who is going through grief, we need to be sensitive to the fact that his or her grief must be expressed. Be available as a listener. And don't be afraid to cry along with your grieving friend.

The grief process typically manifests itself by such symptoms as crying, difficulty in sleeping, and a loss of appetite. You need to also be aware of the wide variety of emotions the bereaved person may go through. Some may feel aggrieved at being "deserted" by their departed loved one, or develop anger toward God. Sometimes there is guilt—perhaps over not taking more seriously the final illness, a harsh word spoken, a withheld blessing, or the neglected "shoulds" of a lifetime of living together.

Later, the grief may turn to deep depression—sometimes even despondency. This is especially the case when friends and family have gone on with their lives and are no longer offering the emotional and spiritual support they did at first. Loneliness may become acute. Help your friend unravel their raging sea of emotions. You may discern the need to direct him or her to obtain counsel from their pastor.

The Ministry of Comfort

One of the reasons you and I can minister to others who are grieving is that we ourselves have gone through grief in our own lives. There have been times when we have grieved at the loss of a loved one, and we have experienced God's great comfort. Now we can be used of God to bring comfort to others.

As the apostle Paul put it in 2 Corinthians 1:3-4, "Praise be to the God and Father of our Lord Jesus Christ, the Father of compassion and the God of all comfort, who comforts us in all our troubles, so that we can comfort those in any trouble with the comfort we ourselves have received from God." Seen in this light, you and I can become a channel of blessing through which God's comfort can flow to the one who hurts.

The Lord Is Our Refuge

Sometimes when a loved one dies, those close to the deceased ask, "Where is God's love and plan in this?" Help the grieving person to see that you and I may not know God's sovereign plan.

But we can take refuge in the fact that we know the Planner. And the Planner—Jesus Christ Himself—knows the meaning of grief. He wept at the funeral of His friend Lazarus. He suffered as all of us suffer when someone dies. And most important, He cares deeply for each one of us. He cares more than we know.

The Scriptures tell us that "the LORD is close to the broken-hearted and saves those who are crushed in spirit" (Psalm 34:18). Truly it is the Lord who is our refuge when a loved one dies. He Himself is our balm. And the Lord often brings His comfort to us through the pages of Scripture. Bible verses you may want to share with your grieving friend or family member include the following:

- "The LORD himself goes before you and will be with you; he will never leave you nor forsake you. Do not be afraid; do not be discouraged" (Deuteronomy 31:8).

- "The LORD is my rock, my fortress and my deliverer; my God is my rock, in whom I take refuge. He is my shield and the horn of my salvation, my stronghold" (Psalm 18:2).

- "God is our refuge and strength, an ever-present help in trouble" (Psalm 46:1).

- "He alone is my rock and my salvation; he is my fortress, I shall never be shaken" (Psalm 62:2).

- "Blessed are those who mourn, for they will be comforted" (Matthew 5:4).

- "I am the living bread that came down from heaven. If anyone eats of this bread, he will live forever. This bread is my flesh, which I will give for the life of the world" (John 6:51).

- "When Jesus spoke again to the people, he said, 'I am the light of the world. Whoever follows me will never walk in darkness, but will have the light of life'" (John 8:12).

- "Jesus said to her, 'I am the resurrection and the life. He who believes in me will live, even though he dies'" (John 11:25).

- "My God will meet all your needs according to his glorious riches in Christ Jesus" (Philippians 4:19).

- "Let us then approach the throne of grace with confidence, so that we may receive mercy and find grace to help us in our time of need" (Hebrews 4:16).

- "We fix our eyes not on what is seen, but on what is unseen. For what is seen is temporary, but what is unseen is eternal" (2 Corinthians 4:18).

Going On with Life

After time passes by—during which months of grief seem to have overshadowed everything—eventually there comes a point when life isn't so painful. In the book *Grief and How to Live with It*, Sharan Morris says, "Finally, a remarkable thing begins to happen. You notice that for short periods the hurt is not so great. This is the beginning of your healing."[7] The Lord will sustain a person not only through his or her initial grief, but He will also help that person become whole again. *He is faithful.*

A key goal in ministering to people who grieve is to help them gain an eternal perspective that will enable them to move beyond their grief to get on with their life. I will address the issue of an eternal perspective in chapter 13. For now, I close with some words from a father who gave some important counsel to his daughter on the first anniversary of her mother's death.

"I had forty wonderful years with your Mom," he said, "the best years of my life. But that part of my life is over. Finished!"

"But Dad..."

"No buts, listen to me."

His clear blue eyes stared intensely into mine. I couldn't turn away from him, as much as I wanted to.

"They were the best years of my life," he repeated. "Your mother is no longer with me; this truth has to be faced. But I am alive and must live the time allotted me until she and I are together again."

His voice trembled, but it was not uncertain.

"She is gone," he said, "but no one can take away the wonderful memories. They are part of me, the happy memories and the sad ones. But only a part. I can't let them possess me or I couldn't get through my days. Every day is a gift from God. It must be lived with joy. It is just a taste of the joy to come when we will all be together again."

I kissed him then, not realizing that our conversation would one day be one of my fondest memories. Recalling that day has always been a great strength to me, particularly today—the first anniversary of my dear father's death.[8]

13

LOOKING TOWARD ETERNITY

The Bible begins with *paradise lost,* at which time pain, suffering, and death first entered the human race. The Bible ends with *paradise regained,* at which time pain, suffering, and death will be a thing of the past.

Once we are in heaven, the sufferings we experienced during our time on earth—even extreme suffering—will be viewed as a momentary bother. As Saint Teresa put it, "In light of heaven, the worst suffering on earth, a life full of the most atrocious tortures on earth, will be seen to be no more serious than one night in an inconvenient hotel."[1] Theologian John Wenham comments, "Not only is it certain that this life will end, but it is certain that from the perspective of eternity it will be seen to have passed in a flash. The toils which seem so endless will be seen to have been quite transitory and abundantly worthwhile."[2] It is with this in mind that Christian writer Philip Yancey comments: "In the Christian scheme of things, this world and the time spent here are not all there is. Earth is a proving ground, a dot in eternity."[3]

In the present chapter, I want to narrow our attention to the important subject of maintaining an eternal perspective. I have briefly touched on this previously in the book, but it is appropriate that I expand on this theme in this final chapter. My reason is simple: I believe that such a perspective gives us the strength we need to withstand the punches that life often throws at us during this "dot in eternity." After all, this "dot in eternity" is quickly passing away. It will soon be over. Our destiny in heaven, by contrast, is an *eternal* destiny. We will live there forever, and it will be a pain-free and death-free environment. That is something to look forward to.

The incredible glory of the afterlife should motivate each of us to live faithfully during our relatively short time on earth. Especially when difficult times come, we must remember that we are but pilgrims on our way to another land—to the final frontier of heaven where God Himself dwells.

J.I. Packer once said that the "lack of long, strong thinking about our promised hope of glory is a major cause of our plodding, lack-luster lifestyle."[4] Packer points to the Puritans as a much-needed example for us, for they believed that "it is the heavenly Christian that is the lively Christian."[5] The Puritans understood that we "run so slowly, and strive so lazily, because we so little mind the prize…So let Christians animate themselves daily to run the race set before them by practicing heavenly meditation."[6]

How I have come to appreciate the Puritans! How I personally seek to imitate their example! The Puritans "saw themselves as God's pilgrims, traveling home through rough country; God's warriors, battling the world, the flesh, and the devil; and God's servants, under orders to worship, fellowship, and do all the good they could as they went along."[7] We should have the same kind of attitude.

I am particularly impressed with the writings of Puritan Richard Baxter, author of the classic *Saints' Everlasting Rest.* Truly he had some habits worthy of imitation. His first habit was to "estimate everything—values, priorities, possessions, relationships, claims, tasks—as these things will appear when one actually comes to die."[8] In other words, he weighed everything in terms of eternal benefit. After all, our life on earth is *short*; our life in heaven is *forever.* If we work only for the things of this earth, what eternal benefit will all of it have?

Baxter's second habit was to "dwell on the glory of the heavenly life to which one was going."[9] Baxter daily practiced "holding heaven at the forefront of his thoughts and desires."[10] The hope of heaven brought him joy, and joy brought him strength. Baxter once said, "A heavenly mind is a joyful mind; this is the nearest and truest way to live a life of comfort...A heart in heaven will be a most excellent preservative against temptations, a powerful means to kill thy corruptions."[11] He offered encouragement: "Be of good cheer, Christian, the time is near, when God and thou shalt be near, and as near as thou canst well desire. Thou shalt dwell in his family."[12] What a day to look forward to!

J.C. Ryle, who seems to have been made of the same stuff as Richard Baxter, urged: "Let us not be afraid to meditate often on the subject of heaven, and to rejoice in the prospect of good things to come." Indeed, "Let us take comfort in the remembrance of the other side."[13] We ought to "look up and look forward! The time is short. The world is growing old. The coming of the Lord draweth nigh."[14]

A "Top-down" Perspective

Gary R. Habermas and J.P. Moreland have come up with a

term I like a lot: a "top-down" perspective. That is precisely what we need during our earthly pilgrimage as we sojourn toward the heavenly country:

> The God of the universe invites us to view life and death from his eternal vantage point. And if we do, we will see how readily it can revolutionize our lives: daily anxieties, emotional hurts, tragedies, our responses and responsibilities to others, possessions, wealth, and even physical pain and death. All of this and much more can be informed and influenced by the truths of heaven. The repeated witness of the New Testament is that believers should view all problems, indeed, their entire existence, from what we call the "top-down" perspective: God and his kingdom first, followed by various aspects of our earthly existence.[15]

Heavenly mindedness can help us keep our heads "screwed on straight" as Christians. As Christian leader Mark Buchanan puts it, "Heavenly-mindedness is sanity. It is the best regimen for keeping our hearts whole, our minds clear.... It allows us to endure life's agonies without despair."[16] It can also motivate us to engage in the work that really matters. Indeed, Buchanan says, "Those who have cultivated a genuine heavenly-mindedness— who have named and nurtured the human longing for *Elsewhere* and *Otherwise*—have been people who have worked and prayed the most passionately, courageously, tirelessly, and unswervingly for the kingdom to come on earth as it is in heaven."[17] J. Oswald Sanders agrees, noting, "A study of history, both secular and sacred, reveals that the Christians who have affected the most significant social change have been those who have been gripped by 'the powers of the coming age' (Hebrews 6:5)."[18]

Certainly a top-down perspective comes in handy when life

throws us a punch. I love the way Randy Alcorn says it: "Antici-pating Heaven doesn't eliminate pain, but it lessens it and puts it in perspective. Meditating on Heaven is a great pain reliever. It reminds us that suffering and death are temporary condi-tions." He is *spot on* in his assessment that "the biblical doctrine of Heaven is about *the future,* but it has tremendous benefits *here and now.* If we grasp it, it will shift our center of gravity and radi-cally change our perspective on life."[19]

I recently came across a parable intended to teach that while unbelievers typically interpret all human suffering as something that "just happens," believers can see suffering as something that can help prepare us for the afterlife, and therefore has a good purpose, as guided by God. It is a parable that imagines twins— a brother and a sister—talking to each other in their mother's womb. It goes like this:

> The sister said to the brother, "I believe there is life after birth."
>
> Her brother protested vehemently, "No, no, this is all there is. This is a dark and cozy place, and we have nothing else to do but to cling to the cord that feeds us."
>
> The little girl insisted, "There must be something more than this dark place. There must be something else, a place with light where there is freedom to move." Still, she could not convince her twin brother.
>
> After some silence, the sister said hesitantly, "I have something else to say, and I'm afraid you won't believe that, either, but I think there is a mother."
>
> Her brother became furious. "A mother!" he shouted. "What are you talking about? I have never seen a

mother, and neither have you. Who put that idea in your head? As I told you, this place is all we have. Why do you always want more? This is not such a bad place, after all. We have all we need, so let's be content."

The sister was quite overwhelmed by her brother's response and for a while didn't dare say anything more. But she couldn't let go of her thoughts, and since she had only her twin brother to speak to, she finally said, "Don't you feel these squeezes every once in a while? They're quite unpleasant and sometimes even painful."

"Yes," he answered. "What's special about that?"

"Well," the sister said, "I think that these squeezes are there to get us ready for another place, much more beautiful than this, where we will see our mother face-to-face. Don't you think that's exciting?"

The brother didn't answer. He was fed up with the foolish talk of his sister and felt that the best thing would be simply to ignore her and hope that she would leave him alone.[20]

What a tragedy that so many in our world today mimic the behavior of the hard-hearted brother in regard to what the Bible says about heaven and the afterlife. But for those of us, like the sister, who are believers, and who maintain a top-down perspective, the hard knocks of life—those "pressures"—are tempered by the glorious future that awaits us.

A top-down perspective also helps us to have a balanced perspective on money and wealth. John MacArthur is correct when he says our goals "should not include the accumulation of possessions here. Our real wealth—our eternal reward—is in heaven (Matt. 5:12)."[21] Why, then, do so many Christians spend a lifetime staying busier than a bee, seeking to accumulate material wealth?

They often do so to the detriment of spending quality time with significant others. Ah, my friend, we must be cautious not to be deceived by the enticing allurements of the world which are passing away.

A key passage on the "top-down" perspective is Matthew 6:19-34. Here Jesus informs us that anxiety will not change anything. Certainly it will not increase the length of our lives (see verse 27). Our goal should therefore be to store up treasures in heaven. This will help rid our lives of anxiety. Make note of this principle: *Our hearts will coincide with the placement of our treasures.*

If we are usually anxious over temporal problems, our hearts are likely not centered on what should properly be our first love. If we have *perpetual* anxiety, there is a good possibility that we are more occupied with transient realities than Jesus intended. So, here we have a ready-made test by which we can assess the depth of our beliefs.[22]

Our goal should not only be to attain but to *maintain* a "top-down" perspective. This perspective is a radical love of God that places Him first and foremost in every aspect of our lives. We are to concentrate our concerns on the eternal, not the temporal (2 Corinthians 4:18). And when we do this, God has promised to meet all our earthly needs as part of the package (Matthew 6:33)! *What could be better?*

Set Your Minds on Things Above

In Colossians 3:1-2, we read: "Since, then, you have been raised with Christ, set your hearts on things above, where Christ is seated at the right hand of God. Set your minds on things above, not on earthly things."[23] The original Greek of this passage is intense: "*Diligently, actively, single-mindedly* pursue the things above."[24] It is also a present tense, carrying the idea, "*perpetually keep on* seeking the things above…Make it an *ongoing process.*"[25]

Strong words! I love this passage, and I can tell you that putting the passage into practice can make all the difference in how we live our lives on this temporal earth.

It is highly revealing that the apostle Paul found it necessary to issue this instruction. The implication is that he did so because setting our minds on the things above is not something that happens naturally or all by itself. It is not an automatic process for Christians. In fact, it is quite common in Scripture for commands to be issued *specifically because* we as human beings have a tendency to gravitate toward the precise opposite behavior—in this case, focusing our attention on things below (earth). Because we are unaccustomed to setting our minds on things above, we need to commit anew to it every day.[26]

When you think about it, setting our minds on things above makes good sense. After all, the earth is *temporal.* It is passing away. Heaven is *eternal,* and it lasts *forever.* Why set our minds on that which is fleeting (earth)? It is such an unwise thing to do, and yet so many Christians today seem focused only on the things this world has to offer.

One of the reasons we ought to be setting our minds on things above is that this is where our true citizenship is. As Philippians 3:20 puts it, "Our citizenship is in heaven. And we eagerly await a Savior from there, the Lord Jesus Christ." Alister McGrath has written a little book entitled *A Brief History of Heaven* in which he provides some keen insights about our true citizenship:

> Paul himself was a Roman citizen, who knew what privileges this brought—particularly on those occasions when he found himself in conflict with the Roman authorities. For Paul, Christians possess something greater: the "citizenship of heaven," which is to

be understood as a present possession, not something that is yet to come. While believers have yet to enter into the full possession of what this citizenship entails, they already possess that privilege. We have no permanent citizenship in this world...As the author of the letter to the Hebrews put it, "here we have no lasting city, but we are looking for the city that is to come" (Hebrews 13:14).[27]

We are citizens of heaven. *That* is where we truly belong. *That* is where we are ultimately headed. Meanwhile, we are "strangers and exiles on the earth" (Hebrews 11:13 NASB). We are pilgrims en route to the heavenly country (verse 16). This in itself can be a source of strength when life gets tough. Christian scholar Arnold Fruchtenbaum urges,

> What that means practically is that all trials and tribulations in this life do not need to be taken to the point of defeat or to the point of despair or to the point of depression. Rather, believers can look upon them and say, "This, too, will pass; I am only a temporary resident on this earth, in this land. This, too, will pass. My citizenship is in heaven. I will some day know the full joy of the Lord."[28]

Hope That Fuels Faith

Our hope in the future glory of the afterlife fuels our faith in the present. Hope and faith—these are closely tied to each other in the pages of Scripture. The apostle Paul tells us that faith involves "being sure of what we hope for" (Hebrews 11:1).

In his classic *Institutes of the Christian Religion*, John Calvin delineated for us how hope relates to faith: "Hope refreshes faith, that it may not become weary. It sustains faith to the final goal, that it may not fail in midcourse, or even at the starting gate. In short, by unremitting renewing and restoring, it invigorates faith again and again with perseverance."[29]

One of my favorite Old Testament characters is Moses. His life vividly illustrates how hope can feed and sustain faith:

> By faith Moses, when he had grown up, refused to be known as the son of Pharaoh's daughter. He chose to be mistreated along with the people of God rather than to enjoy the pleasures of sin for a short time. He regarded disgrace for the sake of Christ as of greater value than the treasures of Egypt, because *he was looking ahead to his reward.* By faith he left Egypt, not fearing the king's anger; *he persevered because he saw him who is invisible*" (Hebrews 11:24-27, emphasis added).

Moses could have had immeasurable power, authority, and riches had he chosen to stay in Egypt. Yet he gave it all up because of his faith in God. He perceived another King, another kingdom. His faith was nourished by his hope of a future reward, a hope of living in the eternal city with the living Lord of the universe, a hope that gave him an eternal perspective.

Truly our faith enables us to perceive the eternal. I very much like John Wesley's insights on this subject:

> True Christian faith fulfills man's desires to perceive the eternal. It gives him a more extensive knowledge of all things invisible. Living faith introduces him to what the eye has not seen, nor the ear heard, nor the heart conceived in the clearest light, with the fullest certainty and evidence. Knowing these benefits, who would not wish for such a faith? With faith comes not only this awareness, but also the fulfillment of the promise of holiness and happiness.[30]

So, then, walking by sight we behold disease, decay, and death as regular features of our world. Walking by faith, however, enables us to see the reality beyond the physical senses into the world of the eternal. Walking by faith enables us to be sure of our future destiny. And, as we have seen throughout this book, the destiny of those who believe in Jesus Christ is a wonderful destiny indeed. For we will live forever with Christ in resurrected bodies that will never again be susceptible to disease, decay, and death. Let our faith cause us to rejoice in this!

The great preacher Charles Spurgeon once said, "A little faith will bring your soul to heaven; a great faith will bring heaven to your soul."[31] One of the ways faith brings heaven to our souls relates to the realization of a heavenly destiny with Christ. Such faith rests in the assurance that regardless of what happens on this puny speck-of-a-planet, our destiny is the eternal city, the heavenly country, at the very side of Christ. So, like Peter on the water, let us look more steadily at Jesus, and less at the waves and wind in our lives. Scripture says that God "will keep in perfect peace him whose mind is steadfast, because he trusts in [God]" (Isaiah 26:3). Let us keep our steadfast gaze heavenward!

Death Holds No Fear, for It Is Conquered

An eternal perspective is one which recognizes that we no longer need fear death, for it has been conquered. As the psalmist said, "Even though I walk through the valley of the shadow of death, I will fear no evil, for you are with me; your rod and your staff, they comfort me" (Psalm 23:4). The same is taught in the New Testament (see 1 Corinthians 15:51-57; 2 Corinthians 5:1-8). Theologian Wayne Grudem is right when he says, "The New Testament encourages us to view our own death not with fear but with joy at the prospect of going to be with Christ."[32] J. Oswald Sanders says, "Death should not be viewed as a *terminus* but as a *tunnel* leading into an ampler and incredibly more wonderful and beautiful world. The death of a believer is a transition, not a final condition."[33]

Certainly the apostle Paul had no fear of death. He affirmed without hesitation, "I desire to depart and be with Christ, which is better by far" (Philippians 1:23). When Paul said heaven was better *by far,* he was speaking from experience, for he had previously been caught up to heaven and was thus a firsthand witness of what lies in our future (2 Corinthians 12:2-4). As Sanders puts it, "When the hour of his martyrdom drew near, he faced it with a cheerful serenity and sublime assurance. There was no fear or reluctance."[34]

Let us rejoice that when Christians pass through death's door, neither pain nor death will ever be faced by them again, for God "will wipe every tear from their eyes. There will be no more death or mourning or crying or pain, for the old order of things has passed away" (Revelation 21:4). J. Sidlow Baxter provides us with this encouragement:

> Your last breath here will instantaneously give place to deathless life, complete healing, and exquisite joy there. The last earthly shadow will melt in the cloudless glory-light of a better world. What we call "the valley of the shadow" here on this side is so bright with light from the other side, that as soon as we enter it, darkness vanishes.... For Christians, death on its earthward side is simply that the tired mortal body falls temporarily to sleep, while on the heavenward side we suddenly find ourselves with our dear Savior-King and with other Christian loved ones in the heavenly home. *Why fear that?*[35]

Hermann Lange's life perfectly illustrates what it means to

live with the attitude Baxter portrays above. Lange was a young German preacher who stood among the Christians who spoke out against Adolf Hitler's repression of the gospel. Like many others, Lange was arrested, interrogated, tried as a criminal, and condemned to die before a firing squad. On the last day of his life he wrote a farewell letter to his parents:

> When this letter comes to your hands, I shall no longer be among the living. The thing that has occupied our thoughts constantly for many months, never leaving them free, is now about to happen.

> If you ask me what state I am in, I can only answer: I am, first, in a joyous mood, and second, filled with great anticipation. As regards the first feeling, today means the end of all suffering and all earthly sorrow for me—and "God will wipe away every tear" from my eyes. What consolation, what marvelous strength emanates from faith in Christ, who has preceded us in death. In him, I have put my faith, and precisely today I have faith in him more firmly than ever….

> And as to the second feeling [of anticipation], this day brings the greatest hour of my life! Everything that till now I have done, struggled for, and accomplished has at bottom been directed to this one goal, whose barrier I shall penetrate today. "Eye hath not seen, nor ear heard, neither have entered into the heart of man, the things which God hath prepared for them that love him" (1 Corinthians 2:9)….

> Until we meet again above in the presence of the Father of Light,

> Your joyful Hermann.[36]

Dear friends, because of what Jesus has done for us, we too can approach death with the same fearlessness as joyful Hermann. As I close this chapter, I urge you to prayerfully meditate on the wonderful lyrics of one of my favorite hymns: "My Jesus I Love Thee," written by William R. Featherstone. Consciously allow these lyrics to saturate your soul and draw your attention to the things above:

> My Jesus, I love Thee, I know Thou art mine;
> > For Thee all the follies of sin I resign.
> My gracious Redeemer, my Savior art Thou;
> > If ever I loved Thee, my Jesus, 'tis now.
>
> I love Thee because Thou has first loved me,
> > And purchased my pardon on Calvary's tree.
> I love Thee for wearing the thorns on Thy brow;
> > If ever I loved Thee, my Jesus, 'tis now.
>
> I'll love Thee in life, I will love Thee in death,
> > And praise Thee as long as Thou lendest
> > me breath;
> And say when the death dew lies cold on my brow,
> > If ever I loved Thee, my Jesus, 'tis now.
>
> In mansions of glory and endless delight,
> > I'll ever adore Thee in heaven so bright;
> I'll sing with the glittering crown on my brow;
> > If ever I loved Thee, my Jesus, 'tis now.

Amen!

POSTSCRIPT—
AN INVITATION TO BELIEVE

D ear reader, there is nothing a person can do to *earn* salvation from God. I am reminded of the fact that in June, 2006, Warren Buffet—the world's second-richest man—announced he was donating 85 percent of his massive $44 billion fortune to five charitable foundations. He commented: "There is more than one way to get to heaven, but this is a great way."[1] While Buffet is to be commended for his tremendous generosity, the truth is that no one—*not even the richest people in the world*—can buy a ticket to heaven. That comes only by a personal relationship with Jesus Christ.

Do *you* have a personal relationship with Jesus Christ? Most of you probably do. But perhaps some of you do not. And perhaps you—after reading in this book of the joys of spending eternity with Jesus in heaven—are now desiring that relationship. It is for you that I have written this postscript.

Entering into a personal relationship with Jesus is the most important decision you could ever make in your life. It is unlike any other relationship. For if you go into eternity without *this* relationship, you will spend eternity apart from Him.

So, if you will allow me, I'd like to tell you how you can come into a personal relationship with Jesus.

First you need to recognize that…

God Desires a Personal Relationship with You

God created you (Genesis 1:27). And He did not just create you to exist all alone and apart from Him. He created you with a view to coming into a personal relationship with Him.

Remember, God had face-to-face encounters and fellowship with Adam and Eve, the first couple (Genesis 3:8-19). And just as God had fellowship with them, so He desires to fellowship with you (1 John 1:5-7). God loves you (John 3:16).

Never forget that fact.

The problem is…

Humanity Has a Sin Problem that Blocks a Relationship with God

When Adam and Eve chose to sin against God in the Garden of Eden, they catapulted the entire human race—to which they gave birth—into sin. Since the time of Adam and Eve, every human being has been born into the world with a propensity to sin.

The apostle Paul affirmed that "sin entered the world through one man, and death through sin" (Romans 5:12). Indeed, we are told that "through the disobedience of the one man the many were made sinners" (Romans 5:19). Ultimately this means that "death came through a man…in Adam all die" (1 Corinthians 15:21-22).

Jesus often spoke of sin in metaphors that illustrate the havoc sin can wreak in one's life. He described sin as blindness (Matthew 23:16-26), sickness (Matthew 9:12), being enslaved in bondage (John 8:34), and living in darkness (John 8:12; 12:35-46).

Jesus also taught that both inner thoughts and external acts render a person guilty before God (Matthew 5:28). He taught that from within the human heart come evil thoughts, sexual immorality, theft, murder, adultery, greed, malice, deceit, lewdness, envy, slander, arrogance, and folly (Mark 7:21-23). Moreover, He affirmed that God is fully aware of every person's sins, both external acts and inner thoughts; nothing escapes His notice (Matthew 22:18; Luke 6:8; John 4:17-19).

Of course, some people are more morally upright than others. But we all fall short of God's infinite standards (Romans 3:23). In a contest to see who can throw a rock to the moon, I am sure a muscular athlete would be able to throw the rock much further than I could. But all human beings ultimately fall short of the task. Similarly, all of us fall short of measuring up to God's perfect holy standards.

Though the sin problem is a serious one, God has graciously provided a solution…

Jesus Died for Our Sins and Made Salvation Possible

God's absolute holiness demands that sin be punished. The good news of the gospel, however, is that Jesus has taken this punishment on Himself. God loves us so much that He sent Jesus to bear the penalty for our sins!

Jesus affirmed that it was for the very purpose of dying that He came into the world (John 12:27). Moreover, He perceived His death as being a sacrificial offering for the sins of humanity (Matthew 26:26-28). Jesus took His sacrificial mission with utmost seriousness, for He knew that without Him, humanity would certainly perish (Matthew 16:25; John 3:16) and spend eternity apart from God in a place of great suffering (Matthew 10:28; 11:23; 23:33; 25:41; Luke 16:22-28).

Jesus therefore described His mission this way: "The Son of Man did not come to be served, but to serve, and to give his life as a ransom for many" (Matthew 20:28). "The Son of Man came to seek and to save what was lost" (Luke 19:10). "God did not send his Son into the world to condemn the world, but to save the world through him" (John 3:17).

But the benefits of Christ's death on the cross are not automatically applied to your life. *God requires you to...*

Believe in Jesus Christ

By His sacrificial death on the cross, Jesus took the sins of the entire world on Himself and made salvation available for everyone (1 John 2:2). But this salvation is not automatic. Only those who personally choose to believe in Christ are saved. This is the consistent testimony of the biblical Jesus. Consider His words:

- "For God so loved the world that he gave his one and only Son, that whoever believes in him shall not perish but have eternal life" (John 3:16).

- "I tell you the truth, whoever hears my word and believes him who sent me has eternal life and will not be condemned; he has crossed over from death to life" (John 5:24).

- "For my Father's will is that everyone who looks to the Son and believes in him shall have eternal life, and I will raise him up at the last day" (John 6:40).

- "I am the resurrection and the life. He who believes in me will live, even though he dies" (John 11:25).

Choosing *not* to believe in Jesus, by contrast, leads to eternal condemnation: "Whoever believes in him is not condemned, but whoever *does not* believe stands condemned already because he has not believed in the name of God's one and only Son" (John 3:18, emphasis added).

In view of such facts, J.C. Ryle exhorts, "The Lord Jesus Christ is able and ready to save you: why not commit your soul to Him, and lay hold of the hand which He holds out from heaven?"[2] Believe in Him today and *you will have eternal life!*

Free At Last: Forgiven of All Sins

When you believe in Christ the Savior, a wonderful thing happens. God forgives you of all your sins. *All of them!* He puts them completely out of His sight. Ponder for a few minutes the following verses, which speak of the forgiveness of those who have believed in Christ:

- "In him we have redemption through his blood, the forgiveness of sins, in accordance with the riches of God's grace" (Ephesians 1:7).

- God said, "Their sins and lawless acts I will remember no more" (Hebrews 10:17-18).

- "Blessed is he whose transgressions are forgiven, whose sins are covered. Blessed is the man whose sin the LORD does not count against him and in whose spirit is no deceit" (Psalm 32:1-2).

- "For as high as the heavens are above the earth, so great is his love for those who fear him; as far as the east is from the west, so far has he removed our transgressions from us" (Psalm 103:11-12).

Look at that last verse again. There is a definite point that is north and another that is south—the North and South Poles. But there are no such points for east and west.

It does not matter how far you go to the east; you will never arrive where east begins because by definition east is the opposite of west. The two never meet. They never will meet and never could meet because they are defined as opposites.

To remove our sins "as far as the east is from the west" is by definition to put them where *no one can ever find them.* That is the forgiveness God has granted us.

Though it may be hard for us to understand, God is able to *forget* our past. God throws our sins into the depths of the sea and puts up a sign on the shore that reads, "No fishing."

Such forgiveness is wonderful indeed, for none of us can possibly work our way into heaven, or be good enough to warrant God's good favor. Because of what Jesus has done for us, we freely receive the gift of salvation. It is a gift provided solely through the grace of God (Ephesians 2:8-9). And all of it is ours by simply believing in Jesus.

Don't Put It Off

It is a highly dangerous thing to put off turning to Christ for salvation, for you do not know the day of your death. What if it happens this evening? "Death is the destiny of every man; the living should take this to heart" (Ecclesiastes 7:2).

If God is speaking to your heart now, then now is your door of opportunity to believe. "Seek the LORD while he may be found; call on him while he is near" (Isaiah 55:6). The apostle Paul emphasized that "now is the day of salvation" (2 Corinthians 6:2).

Follow Me in Prayer

Would you like to place your faith in Jesus for the forgiveness of sins, thereby guaranteeing your eternal place in heaven along His side? If so, pray the following prayer with me.

Keep in mind that it is not the prayer itself that saves you. It is the faith in your heart that saves you. So, let the following prayer be a simple expression of the faith that is in your heart:

> *Dear Jesus:*
> *I want to have a relationship with You.*
> *I know I can't save myself, because I know*
>   *I am a sinner.*
> *Thank you for dying on the cross on my behalf.*
> *I believe You died for me, and I accept Your*
>   *free gift of salvation.*
>
>   *Thank You, Jesus.*
>   *Amen.*

Welcome to God's Forever Family

On the authority of the Word of God, I can now assure you that you are a part of God's forever family. If you prayed the above prayer with a heart of faith, you will spend all eternity by the side of Jesus in heaven. Welcome to God's family!

If you have just become a Christian, I want to help you. I would like to send you some free materials that will help you grow in your faith.

If you are already a Christian, I would like to hear from you too. I have many materials that will help you mature as a Christian.

Please write:

Ron Rhodes
Reasoning from the Scriptures Ministries
P.O. Box 2526
Frisco, TX 75034

God bless you!

APPENDIXES

APPENDIX A

Inspiring Bible Promises on Death, Heaven, and the Afterlife

God has provided many wonderful and comforting Bible promises relating to death, heaven, and the afterlife. In this brief appendix, I invite you to drink richly from these promises of God. May the Lord encourage you and bless you through these promises!

As a helpful Bible study aid, you will notice that key insights of biblical words follow each verse. These words are italicized in the text. The insights are based on the original Hebrew (for Old Testament verses) or the original Greek (for New Testament verses).

God is our guide to the very end of our lives.
This God is our God for ever and ever; he will be our guide even to the *end*.

—Psalm 48:14

end—death

Our bodies may age, but our spirits are renewed.
We do not *lose heart*. Though outwardly we are *wasting away*, yet inwardly we are *being renewed* day by day.

—2 Corinthians 4:16

lose heart—give up, become discouraged, become wearied
wasting away—progressively decaying (in our physical
   bodies)
being renewed—continually and perpetually renewed

God will one day abolish death.

He will *swallow up* death forever. The Sovereign LORD will *wipe
away* the tears from all faces.

   —Isaiah 25:8

swallow up—consume, devour, gulp down
wipe away—blot out, exterminate

God will abolish tears and death.

He will *wipe* every tear from their eyes. There will be *no more*
death or mourning or crying or pain, for the old order of things
has passed away.

   —Revelation 21:4

wipe—blot out, exterminate
no more—absolutely no more

The death of Christians is precious to God.

Precious in the sight of the LORD is the death of his *saints*.

   —Psalm 116:15

precious—important, valuable
saints—holy ones, godly ones (Christians)

Those who follow Jesus never permanently die.

I tell you the truth, if anyone *keeps* my word, he will never *see
death*.

   —John 8:51

keeps—guards, obeys, observes
see—experience
death—permanent end of life

Death will be swallowed up in victory.

When the perishable has been clothed with the imperishable, and the mortal with immortality, then the saying that is written will come true: "Death has been *swallowed up* in victory."

—1 Corinthians 15:54

swallowed up—overwhelmed, drowned

God comforts those who mourn.

Blessed are those who *mourn*, for they will be *comforted*.

—Matthew 5:4

blessed—happy, joyful, favored by God
mourn—grieve
comforted—encouraged, exhorted

God comforts us in our hurts.

Praise be to the God and Father of our Lord Jesus Christ, the Father of *compassion* and the God of all *comfort,* who comforts us in all our *troubles,* so that we can comfort those in any trouble with the comfort we ourselves have received from God.

—2 Corinthians 1:3-4

compassion—mercy, pity
comfort—consolation, encouragement
troubles—distresses, tribulations

Death cannot separate us from Christ.

I am convinced that neither death nor life, neither angels nor demons, neither the present nor the future, nor any powers, neither height nor depth, nor anything else in all creation, will be able to *separate us* from the *love* of God that is in Christ Jesus our Lord.

—Romans 8:38-39

separate us—divide us, set us apart
love—active love

Death is not the end.

We do not want you to be ignorant about those who *fall asleep*, or to *grieve* like the rest of men, who have no hope.... The dead in Christ will rise first. After that, we who are still alive and are left will be caught up together with them in the clouds to meet the Lord in the air. And so we will be with the Lord forever.

—1 Thessalonians 4:13-17

fall asleep—sleep in death
grieve—be sorrowful, distressed, sad, mournful

Permanent resurrection bodies await us.

We know that if the earthly *tent* we live in is *destroyed*, we have a *building* from God, an eternal house in heaven, not built by human hands.

—2 Corinthians 5:1

tent—mortal body
destroyed—thrown down, dissolved, abolished
building—resurrection body

Those who believe in Jesus will be resurrected.

Jesus said to her, "I am the resurrection and the life. He who *believes in* me will live, even though he dies; and whoever lives and believes in me will never die."

—John 11:25-26

believes in—trusts in, puts faith in, relies on

We have a living hope of resurrection.

Praise be to the God and Father of our Lord Jesus Christ! In his *great mercy* he has given us new birth into a living *hope* through the resurrection of Jesus Christ from the dead.

—1 Peter 1:3

great mercy—superabundant compassion
hope—expectation

Our perishable bodies will be made imperishable.

The body that is *sown* is *perishable,* it is raised *imperishable;* it is sown in *dishonor,* it is raised in glory; it is sown in *weakness,* it is raised in power; it is sown a natural body, it is raised a spiritual body.

—1 Corinthians 15:42-44

sown—scattered in death
perishable—does not last
imperishable—immortal, lasting forever
dishonor—shame, disgrace
weakness—infirmity, illness

A wonderful destiny awaits those who love God.

No eye has *seen,* no ear has heard, no mind has conceived what God has prepared for those who *love* him.

—1 Corinthians 2:9

seen—perceived
love—actively having affection for

We will live with God face-to-face.

Now the *dwelling* of God is with men, and he will *live* with them. They will be his people, and God himself will be with them and be their God. He will *wipe* every tear from their eyes. There will be no more death or *mourning* or crying or pain, for the old order of things has passed away.

> —Revelation 21:3-4

dwelling—abode, tent, tabernacle, shelter
live—encamp
wipe—blot out, exterminate, cancel
mourning—grief, sadness

Our citizenship is in heaven.

Our citizenship is in heaven. And we eagerly await a Savior from there, the Lord Jesus Christ, who, by the *power* that enables him to bring everything under his *control,* will *transform* our lowly bodies so that they will be like his glorious body.

> —Philippians 3:20-21

power—energy
control—subjection, subordination
transform—change the form of, fashion anew

We are destined for glory.

When Christ, who is your life, appears, then you also will *appear* with him in glory.

> —Colossians 3:4

appear—be revealed, be made known, be displayed

Our sufferings pale in comparison to our future glory.

I consider that our present *sufferings* are not worth comparing with the glory that will be revealed in us.

> —Romans 8:18

sufferings—misfortunes

Our future glory outweighs all present troubles.

Our *light* and momentary *troubles* are *achieving* for us an eternal glory that far outweighs them all. So we *fix our eyes* not on what is seen, but on what is unseen. For what is seen is temporary, but what is unseen is eternal.

   —2 Corinthians 4:17-18

light—not burdensome
troubles—distresses, tribulations
achieving—accomplishing, bringing about, producing
fix our eyes—continually focus on

All needs will be met in heaven.

Never again will they hunger; *never again* will they thirst. The sun will not beat upon them, nor any scorching heat. For the Lamb at the center of the throne will be their shepherd; he will lead them to springs of living water. And God will *wipe away* every tear from their eyes.

   —Revelation 7:16-17

never again—not in the slightest degree
wipe away—blot out, exterminate

We will dwell in a new heaven and a new earth.

Then I saw a new heaven and a new earth, for the first heaven and the first earth had *passed away,* and there was no longer any sea. I saw the Holy City, the new Jerusalem, coming down out of heaven from God, prepared as a bride beautifully *dressed* for her husband.

   —Revelation 21:1-2

passed away—vanished
dressed—adorned

In keeping with his promise we are *looking forward* to a new heaven and a new earth, the home of righteousness.

—2 Peter 3:13

looking forward—expectantly waiting for

Our inheritance can never perish, spoil, or fade.
In his great mercy he has given us new birth into a living hope through the resurrection of Jesus Christ from the dead, and into an inheritance that can never *perish,* spoil or fade—*kept* in heaven for you.

—1 Peter 1:3-4

perish—fade away, pass away
kept—guarded

We have an inheritance from the Lord as a reward.
Whatever you do, work at it with all your heart, as working for the Lord, not for men, since you know that you will receive an inheritance from the Lord as a reward. It is the Lord Christ you are *serving.*

—Colossians 3:23-24

serving—being in bondage as a voluntary slave

APPENDIX B

The "Great Cloud of Witnesses": Are We Being Watched from Heaven?

Hebrews 11 and 12 are two chapters that carry high relevance for those looking forward to God's rewards in heaven. In Hebrews 11, we find the Faith Hall of Fame, with many of God's greatest saints being lauded for their faith—people like Enoch, Abel, Noah, Abraham, Isaac, Jacob, Joseph, Moses, and others. Then, in Hebrews 12:1, we read: "Therefore, since we are surrounded by such a *great cloud of witnesses*, let us throw off everything that hinders and the sin that so easily entangles, and let us run with perseverance the race marked out for us" (emphasis added).

People often ask me about this verse, and there are two primary views to consider. The first view holds that there are those in heaven—not just the superheroes of the faith mentioned in Hebrews 11, but also Christian family members and friends who have gone to heaven—who are watching us on earth, looking over heaven's balcony to observe our behavior. They are said to be like "spectators in a vast arena" who "watch us progress."[1] It is thus suggested that this ought to be an incentive to holy living—something that will subsequently increase our rewards once we get to heaven.

In support of the idea that the saints in heaven are aware of things on earth is that the witnesses of Hebrews 11 are said to "surround" us, not merely to have preceded us or gone before us.[2] Further, when Samuel the prophet, following his death, appeared to King Saul, he seemed to be aware of the events in Saul's life (1 Samuel 28:16-18). Likewise, Luke 9:31 tells us that Moses and Elijah "appeared in glorious splendor, talking with Jesus. They spoke about his departure, which he was about to bring to fulfillment at Jerusalem." They seemed to be "in the know" regarding events transpiring on earth relating to Christ's upcoming departure from earth (resurrection and ascension). Moreover, the angels in heaven seem to know what is going on in the earthly realm (see 1 Corinthians 4:9), and if angels know, why not redeemed humans? We are also told that there is "more rejoicing in heaven over one sinner who repents than over ninety-nine righteous persons who do not need to repent" (Luke 15:7). It is suggested that this "rejoicing" could include not just angels but also Christians who have already gone to heaven. Further, the Christian martyrs mentioned in Revelation 6:9-10 are aware of the circumstances of their persecutors on earth. Finally, those in heaven who are mentioned in Revelation 19:1-6 are aware that Babylon has been destroyed on earth.[3]

So, it is reasoned, because the saints in heaven are watching events on earth, we ought to be careful to live right. When Christian philosopher Peter Kreeft was asked what difference Hebrews 12:1 should make in how we live our lives, he replied: "What difference does this make? Well, what difference does it make to you if you believe you are being watched by a thousand living human eyes?"[4]

While this may seem a compelling case, other Christians suggest that it may be reading too much into Hebrews 12:1 to conclude that there are saints looking over heaven's balcony, observing our specific behavior. First, there are other possible explanations for the verses cited above. For example, Samuel was a prophet of God, and it is quite possible (even likely) that God personally informed him of Saul's circumstances before He caused Samuel to appear to Saul. The rejoicing in heaven over those who convert on earth could result, not from saints looking over heaven's balcony, but from regular evangelism reports being issued in heaven—like a celestial newscast from the throne room. The same could be true regarding the martyrs in Revelation 6 and those in Revelation 19 who become aware that Babylon has been destroyed. Moreover, a case could be made that if Christians in heaven were looking over the balcony at earth, how could there be no more mourning or tears in heaven, since horrific things occur on a minute-by-minute basis on earth?

Many thus believe that the main idea of Hebrews 12:1 is that because we have been *preceded* by superheroes of the faith (great "witnesses" or "testifiers"), we should seek to mimic their behavior, following their lead in righteous, godly behavior. One commentator writes of these witnesses, "This [verse] does not mean that they are spectators of what goes on earth. Rather they witness *to us* by their lives of faith and endurance and set a high standard for us to duplicate."[5]

When you think about it, the primary incentive for us to live righteously is that *God Himself* is observing us—and it is before *Him* that we must one day appear to give an account (1 Corinthians 3:10-15; 2 Corinthians 5:10). Therefore, as the writer of Hebrews exhorts, "let us throw off everything that hinders and the sin that so easily entangles, and let us run with perseverance the race marked out for us." Moreover, "Let us fix our eyes on Jesus, the author and perfecter of our faith" (Hebrews 12:1-2).

APPENDIX C

Assessing Alleged Firsthand
Reports About Heaven

In this book, the Bible has been our sole authority on all matters pertaining to death, heaven, and the afterlife. Today, however, many claim to have actually visited heaven during a so-called "near-death experience." In many such cases, people are providing firsthand reports of what they witnessed. Should such reports be trusted?

Following are some primary considerations:

The Apostle Paul "Not Permitted to Speak"

The Bible tells us that when the apostle Paul was caught up to the third heaven (paradise), he heard "inexpressible words, which a man *is not permitted to speak*" (2 Corinthians 12:4, emphasis added). One must therefore ask: If God forbade Paul to speak of the things he witnessed in heaven, why would God allow dozens of modern people—who are not even apostles like Paul was—to speak of what they witnessed, and inform us of things not corroborated by the Bible?[1]

A Warning in the Book of Revelation

Much of what we learn about heaven is found in the Book of

Revelation. After John received this revelation from God, God warned that no one should *add* words or *take away* words from what is written (Revelation 22:18-19). People today who claim to have been to heaven and back, writing sensational books that are full of new revelations about heaven, come perilously close to violating the spirit of this passage.[2]

False Doctrines from the "Being of Light"

It has been claimed by numerous (not all) individuals who have had so-called near-death experiences that they encountered a being of light believed to be Jesus. According to some of these reports, this being says things contrary to the Christ of the Bible, such as the following: (1) Sin is not a problem; (2) there is no hell to worry about; (3) all people are welcome in heaven, regardless of whether they have placed faith in Christ; and (4) all religions are equally valid. Since Jesus is the same yesterday, today, and forever (Hebrews 13:8), it would be impossible that the Jesus of the Bible would say such things. For this reason, I have no alternative but to conclude that many of the people who have had near-death experiences have actually encountered a *counterfeit* Christ.

Near-Death Experiences Not in the Bible

There are some writers, such as near-death researcher Raymond Moody, who claim that near-death experiences can be found in the Bible. Acts 9:3-6 is cited as a prime example, a passage which speaks of Saul falling to the ground and seeing a light from heaven that was Jesus. Sometime later, after Saul (also known as Paul) had become a Christian, he had a discussion with King Agrippa in which he alluded to this same experience (Acts 26:12-18).

Against this interpretation are five primary points:

1. First, most obviously, Paul was quite alive and was nowhere near death. By no stretch of the imagination, then, can this be called a near-death experience.

2. The light literally blinded Paul (Acts 9:8)—something completely unlike a typical near-death experience.

3. In his later discussion with King Agrippa (Acts 26:12-18), Paul never once mentioned anything remotely resembling a near-death experience.

4. Whereas most people are reticent about talking about their near-death experiences, Paul spoke openly and with boldness about his encounter with the living Jesus.

5. Unlike the Jesus of a typical near-death experience, the Jesus Paul encountered commissioned him to evangelize so that people may receive forgiveness of sins by faith in Jesus and thereby escape hell.

We conclude that the Book of Acts contains no references to near-death experiences. The same is true of the rest of the Bible.

The Connection with Occultism

Many researchers have noted a clear connection between near-death experiences and occultism. John Weldon and John Ankerberg, for example, tell us that in large measure the near-death experience is merely one form of the occult out-of-body experience. They note that *both* kinds of experiences typically lead to spiritistic contact, worldview changes, and the development of psychic powers.[3]

In keeping with this, near-death researcher Kenneth Ring has documented that people frequently experience "psychic events" following a near-death experience. He has also noted the claim of many that their "psychic sensitivities have developed strikingly" since their near-death experiences.[4] Others have reported the emergence of clairvoyance and telepathy following such experiences. Some have claimed to encounter a spirit guide.

The obvious problem with all this is that occultism and psychic phenomena are strongly condemned by God in Scripture. Anyone doubting this should meditate on Deuteronomy 18:10-13.

These Are Not *Actual* Deaths

Near-death experiences do not actually prove anything about the *final* state of the dead. After all, these experiences are *near*-death experiences, not *once-and-for-all-completely-dead* experiences. Near-death experiences "may tell us no more about death than someone who has been near Denver—but never within city limits—can tell us about that town. Both NDEs (*near-Denver* and *near-death* experiences) are bereft of certitude...In both cases, more reliable maps are available."[5]

The map for evaluating near-death experiences is, of course, the Bible. Scripture defines death as the separation of the spirit from the body (James 2:26). And true death occurs only once (see Hebrews 9:27).

Must *All* Such Experiences Be Rejected?

As we have seen in this appendix, many accounts of near-death experiences have clear connections with occultism and must be outright rejected. As well, many of the accounts portray a "Jesus" saying things that go against the biblical Jesus. These too must be outright rejected.

However, simply because there are many counterfeit experiences, must we conclude that every single person's experience is with a counterfeit Christ and holds no truth to it? In his discerning article on near-death experiences in the *Christian Research Journal*, researcher Jerry Yamamoto wisely suggests that since near-death experiences "are of a subjective nature, determining their source is largely a speculative venture. With divine, demonic, and several natural factors all meriting considerations, a single, universal explanation for near-death experiences becomes quite risky."[6]

Some Christian researchers suggest that even though we must be extremely cautious on this issue, it is possible that some people may have actually had bona fide near-death experiences with the genuine Jesus. This group would especially include Christians, as well as people who became Christians as a direct result of the encounter.

As Jerry Yamamoto puts it, "If the message and experience of a near-death experience does not distort or conflict with biblical teachings, then we should be careful not to speak against that which resulted in salvation and may have been a genuine work of God." Yamamoto cites a case where he thinks this is in fact what occurred. (A man named Dan became a devout Christian immediately after his near-death experience.[7])

Christian apologists Gary R. Habermas and J.P. Moreland, after an extensive study, conclude that "just as you can't have fake money without real money, so you can't have fake near-death experiences without real ones. You can't counterfeit what doesn't exist."[8] Their point is that even though there are many counterfeit near-death experiences that portray a counterfeit Jesus who preaches a counterfeit message, so there are some genuine near-death experiences in which people may have actually encountered the true Jesus.

My best advice is this: No matter what kind of experience is claimed, always test it against Scripture (see Acts 17:11; 1 Thessalonians 5:21). If anything contradicts the Word of God, it must be outright rejected. Make the Scriptures your sole measuring stick. The Scriptures will keep you on track.

BIBLIOGRAPHY

Abanes, Richard. *Embraced by the Light and the Bible*. Camp Hill, PA: Horizon Books, 1994.

Alcorn, Randy. *Heaven*. Wheaton, IL: Tyndale House, 2004.

Ankerberg, John, and Weldon, John. *The Facts on Life After Death*. Eugene, OR: Harvest House, 1992.

Baxter, J. Sidlow. *The Other Side of Death*. Grand Rapids, MI: Kregel Publications, 1997.

Baxter, Richard. *Saints' Everlasting Rest*. Philadelphia, PA: Lippincott, 1859.

Berkhof, Louis. *Manual of Christian Doctrine*. Grand Rapids, MI: Eerdmans, 1983.

Blanchard, John. *Whatever Happened to Hell?* Durham, England: Evangelical Press, 1993.

Boa, Kenneth and Bowman, Robert. *Sense and Nonsense about Heaven and Hell*. Grand Rapids, MI: Zondervan, 2007.

Buchanan, Mark. *Things Unseen: Living in Light of Forever*. Sisters, OR: Multnomah, 2002.

Calvin, John. *Institutes of the Christian Religion*. Philadelphia, PA: Westminster, 1960.

Connelly, Douglas. *What the Bible Really Says: After Life*. Downers Grove, IL: InterVarsity Press, 1995.

Eadie, Betty. *Embraced by the Light*. Placerville, CA: Gold Leaf Press, 1992.

Elwell, Walter A., ed. *Topical Analysis of the Bible*. Grand Rapids, MI: Baker Book House, 1991.

Erickson, Millard J. *Christian Theology*. Grand Rapids, MI: Baker Book House, 1985.

Groothuis, Doug. *Deceived by the Light*. Eugene, OR: Harvest House, 1995.

Habermas, Gary R., and Moreland, J.P. *Immortality: The Other Side of Death*. Nashville, TN: Nelson, 1992.

Henry, Carl F.H., ed. *Basic Christian Doctrines*. Grand Rapids, MI: Baker Book House, 1983.

Hitchcock, Mark. *55 Answers to Questions About Life After Death*. Sisters, OR: Multnomah, 2005.

Hoekema, Anthony A. *The Bible and the Future*. Grand Rapids, MI: Eerdmans, 1984.

Hoyt, Herman A. *The End Times*. Chicago, IL: Moody, 1969.

Kreeft, Peter. *Everything You Ever Wanted to Know about Heaven*. San Francisco, CA: Ignatius Press, 1999.

Kubler-Ross, Elisabeth. *On Death and Dying*. New York: Macmillan, 1969.

Ladd, George Eldon. *The Last Things*. Grand Rapids, MI: Eerdmans, 1982.

Lotz, Anne Graham. *Heaven: My Father's House*. Nashville, TN: Nelson, 2001.

MacArthur, John. *Because the Time is Near*. Chicago, IL: Moody, 2007.

MacArthur, John. *The Glories of Heaven*. Wheaton, IL: Crossway Books, 1996.

Marsden, George. *Jonathan Edwards: A Life*. New Haven, CT: Yale University Press, 2003.

McGrath, Alister. *A Brief History of Heaven*. Malden, MA: Blackwell, 2003.

Milne, Bruce. *Know the Truth*. Downers Grove, IL: InterVarsity Press, 1982.

Moody, Raymond. *Life After Life*. New York: Bantam Books, 1976.

Moody, Raymond. *Reflections on Life After Life*. New York: Bantam Books, 1978.

Morey, Robert A. *Death and the Afterlife*. Minneapolis, MN: Bethany House, 1984.

Morrow, Barry. *Heaven Observed*. Colorado Springs, CO: NavPress, 2001.

Pache, Rene. *The Future Life*. Chicago, IL: Moody, 1980.

Packer, J.I., ed. *Alive to God: Studies in Spirituality*. Downers Grove, IL: InterVarsity Press, 1992.

Packer, J.I. *Knowing God*. Downers Grove, IL: InterVarsity Press, 1973.

Pentecost, J. Dwight. *Things to Come*. Grand Rapids, MI: Zondervan, 1974.

Rawlings, Maurice. *Beyond Death's Door*. New York: Bantam Books, 1979.

Rhodes, Ron. *Angels Among Us: Separating Truth from Fiction*. Eugene, OR: Harvest House, 1995.

Ring, Kenneth. *Life at Death: A Scientific Investigation of the Near-Death Experience*. New York: Coward, McCann, and Geoghegan, 1980.

Robinson, Haddon W. *Grief*. Grand Rapids, MI: Zondervan, 1976.

Ryle, J.C. *Heaven*. Ross-shire, Great Britain: Christian Focus Publications, 2000.

Ryrie, Charles C. *A Survey of Bible Doctrine.* Chicago, IL: Moody, 1980.

Ryrie, Charles C. *Basic Theology.* Wheaton, IL: Victor Books, 1986.

Sanders, J. Oswald. *Heaven: Better by Far.* Grand Rapids, MI: Discovery House, 1993.

Sauer, Eric. *From Eternity to Eternity.* Grand Rapids, MI: Eerdmans, 1979.

Smith, Wilbur M. *The Biblical Doctrine of Heaven.* Chicago, IL: Moody, 1974.

Tada, Joni Eareckson. *Heaven: Your Real Home.* Grand Rapids, MI: Zondervan, 1995.

Taylor, Rick. *When Life Is Changed Forever.* Eugene, OR: Harvest House, 1992.

Thiessen, Henry Clarence. *Lectures in Systematic Theology.* Grand Rapids, MI: Eerdmans, 1981.

Unger, Merrill F. *Beyond the Crystal Ball.* Chicago, IL: Moody, 1973.

Walvoord, John F., and Chafer, Lewis Sperry. *Major Bible Themes.* Grand Rapids, MI: Zondervan, 1975.

Wesley, John. *The Nature of Salvation.* Minneapolis, MN: Bethany House, 1987.

Wright, Rusty. *The Other Side of Life.* San Bernardino, CA: Here's Life, 1979.

Zodhiates, Spiros. *Life After Death.* Chattanooga, TN: AMG, 1989.

NOTES

Introduction—The Wonder of Heaven

1. Electronic online version of "Hamlet." Produced by The Gutenberg Project.

2. W. MacDonald and A. Farstad, *Believer's Bible Commentary* (Nashville, TN: Nelson, 1997), Logos Bible Software.

3. Mark Buchanan, *Things Unseen: Living in Light of Forever* (Sisters, OR: Multnomah, 2002), p. 11.

4. MacDonald and Farstad.

5. John F. Walvoord and Roy Zuck, *The Bible Knowledge Commentary* (Wheaton, IL: Victor, 1985), Logos Bible Software.

6. John MacArthur, *Because the Time Is Near* (Chicago, IL: Moody, 2007), p. 313.

7. J.C. Ryle, *Heaven* (Ross-shire, Great Britain: Christian Focus Publications, 2000), p. 11.

8. Randy Alcorn, *Heaven* (Wheaton, IL: Tyndale House, 2004), p. xx.

9. Barry Morrow, *Heaven Observed: Glimpses of Transcendence in Everyday Life* (Colorado Springs, CO: NavPress, 2001), p. 93.

10. J. Oswald Sanders, *Heaven: Better By Far* (Grand Rapids, MI: Discovery House, 1993), pp. 58-59.

11. Thomas Ice and Timothy J. Demy, *What the Bible Says About Heaven and Eternity* (Grand Rapids, MI: Kregel, 2000), p. 9.

12. Mark Hitchcock, *55 Answers to Questions about Life after Death* (Sisters, OR: Multnomah, 2005), p. 9.

13. J. Boudreau, *The Happiness of Heaven* (Rockford, IL: Tan Books and Publishers, 1984), pp. 2-3.

14. See Arnold Fruchtenbaum, *The Footsteps of the Messiah* (San Antonio, TX: Ariel Press, 1982), p. 749.

15. Hitchcock, p. 13.

16. Martyn Lloyd-Jones, *More Gathered Gold*. Electronic HyperCard database version.

17. See Hitchcock, p. 22.

18. Michael Green, ed. *Bible Illustrations for Preaching.* HyperCard database.

19. David C. Needham, *Birthright: Christian, Do You Know Who You Are?* (Sisters, OR: Multnomah, 1981), p. 12.

20. Joni Eareckson Tada, *Heaven: Your Real Home* (Grand Rapids, MI: Zondervan, 1995), p. 15.

21. Tada, p. 110.

Chapter 1—Entering Death's Door

1. Jonathan Edwards, cited in George Marsden, *Jonathan Edwards: A Life* (New Haven, CT: Yale University Press, 2003), p. 27.

2. J.C. Ryle, *Heaven* (Ross-shire, Great Britain: Christian Focus Publications, 2000), p. 20.

3. J. Sidlow Baxter, *The Other Side of Death* (Grand Rapids, MI: Kregel Publications, 1987), p. 22.

4. Randy Alcorn, *Heaven* (Wheaton, IL: Tyndale House, 2004), p. xxi.

5. John Blanchard, *Whatever Happened to Hell?* (Durham, England: Evangelical Press, 1993), p. 47.

6. Bill O'Reilly, *The O'Reilly Factor,* May 13, 1999.

7. Barry Morrow, *Heaven Observed: Glimpses of Transcendence in Everyday Life* (Colorado Springs, CO: NavPress, 2001), p. 95.

8. Morrow, p. 94.

9. "Death," in *The Concise Columbia Encyclopedia* (electronic media © 1994, licensed from Columbia University Press), in *Microsoft Bookshelf.*

10. Blanchard, p. 67.

11. John F. Walvoord and Roy Zuck, *The Bible Knowledge Commentary* (Wheaton, IL: Victor Books, 1985), Logos Bible Software.

12. Dotson Rader, "I Want to Go On Forever," *Parade,* December 9, 2007, pp. 6-8.

13. Cited in Baxter, p. 98.

14. Joni Eareckson Tada, *Heaven: Your Real Home* (Grand Rapids, MI: Zondervan, 1995), p. 201.

15. Anne Graham Lotz, *Heaven: My Father's House* (Nashville, TN: Nelson, 2001), p. 5, emphasis added.

16. See J. Oswald Sanders, *Heaven: Better By Far* (Grand Rapids, MI: Discovery House, 1993), p. 28.

Chapter 2—Biblical Portrayals of Death

1. John Blanchard, *Whatever Happened to Hell?* (Durham, England: Evangelical Press, 1993), p. 59.

2. Arnold Fruchtenbaum, *The Footsteps of the Messiah* (San Antonio, TX: Ariel Press, 1982), p. 698.

3. See Fruchtenbaum, p. 720.

4. Wayne Grudem, *Systematic Theology: An Introduction to Biblical Doctrine* (Grand Rapids, MI: Zondervan, 1994), p. 816.

5. W. MacDonald and A. Farstad, *Believer's Bible Commentary* (Nashville, TN: Nelson, 1997), Logos Bible Software.

6. John F. Walvoord and Roy Zuck, *The Bible Knowledge Commentary* (Wheaton, IL: Victor Books, 1985), Logos Bible Software.

7. All the above deathbed statements are found in Paul Lee Tan, *Encyclopedia of 7,700 Illustrations* (Rockville, MD: Assurance, 1985), p. 314.

8. Randy Alcorn, *Heaven* (Wheaton, IL: Tyndale House, 2004), p. xxi.

9. George Marsden, *Jonathan Edwards: A Life* (New Haven, CT: Yale University Press, 2003), p. 51.

10. Jonathan Edwards, cited in Alcorn, p. 5.

11. Jonathan Edwards, cited in Alcorn, p. 28.

12. J. Sidlow Baxter, *The Other Side of Death* (Grand Rapids, MI: Kregel Publications, 1987), p. 8.

13. John MacArthur, *The Glory of Heaven* (Wheaton, IL: Crossway Books, 1996), p. 69.

Chapter 3—Life in the Intermediate State

1. Billy Graham, *Angels: God's Secret Agents* (Garden City, NY: Doubleday, 1975), p. 152.

2. Herman Hoyt, *The End Times* (Chicago, IL: Moody, 1969), p. 46; See also J. Oswald Sanders, *Heaven: Better By Far* (Grand Rapids, MI: Discovery House, 1993), p. 44.

3. Randy Alcorn, *Heaven* (Wheaton, IL: Tyndale House, 2004), p. 57.

4. See Arnold Fruchtenbaum, *The Footsteps of the Messiah* (San Antonio, TX: Ariel Press, 1982), p. 726.

5. Fruchtenbaum, p. 726.

6. See Anthony Hoekema, *The Bible and the Future* (Grand Rapids, MI: Eerdmans, 1984), p. 349.

7. J. Sidlow Baxter, *The Other Side of Death* (Grand Rapids, MI: Kregel, 1987), p. 50.

8. The Tribulation will be a definite period of time at the end of the age that will be characterized by great travail (Matthew 24:29-35). It will be of such severity that no period in history, past or future, will equal it (Matthew 24:21). It is called the time of Jacob's trouble, for it is a judgment on Messiah-rejecting Israel (Jeremiah 30:7; Daniel 12:1-4). The nations will also be judged for their sin and rejection of Christ (Isaiah 26:21; Revelation 6:15-17). The period will last seven years (Daniel 9:24,27). Scripture indicates that this period will be characterized by wrath (Isaiah 26:20-21; Revelation 16:1), judgment (Revelation 14:7), trial (Revelation 3:10), destruction (Joel 1:15), darkness (Amos 5:18), desolation (Daniel 9:27), overturning (Isaiah 24:1-4), and punishment (Isaiah 24:20-21). The term "Tribulation" is hence quite appropriate.

9. Baxter, *The Other Side of Death*, p. 54.

10. *Bible Illustrations for Preaching*, ed. Michael Green, HyperCard database.

11. Moses and Elijah did not have their resurrection bodies, since the day of resurrection is yet future. Some scholars believe they took on some form of temporary manifestation, similar to the way that angels as spirit-beings can take on a temporary appearance.

12. Hoekema, p. 99.

13. Robert Morey, *Death and the Afterlife* (Minneapolis, MN: Bethany House, 1984), p. 86.

14. Charles Ryrie, *Basic Theology* (Wheaton, IL: Victor, 1986), p. 520.

15. John MacArthur, *The Glory of Heaven* (Wheaton, IL: Crossway, 1996), pp. 76-77.

16. MacArthur, p. 78.

17. Ryrie, p. 520.

18. Early in my career I held to the Hades view, as did many of my colleagues. Subsequent Bible study has led me to embrace the Heaven view.

19. Douglas Connelly, *What the Bible Really Says: After Life* (Downers Grove, IL: InterVarsity, 1995), p. 18.

20. In this verse, an aorist infinitive ("to depart") is linked by a single article with a present infinitive ("to be with Christ"). The infinitives thus belong together. The single article ties the two infinitives together, so that the actions depicted by the two infinitives are to be considered two aspects of the same thing, or two sides of the same coin. Hence, Paul is saying in this verse that the very moment after he "departs" the body or dies, he will be with Christ in heaven.

21. Hoekema, p. 356, emphasis added.

22. Hoekema, p. 356, insert added.

23. Hoekema, p. 356.

24. "Today in the Word," *Illustrations*, Dallas Theological Seminary, April 10, 1993.

25. Morey, p. 86.

26. Hoekema, p. 102.

Chapter 4—Alive Forevermore: The Future Resurrection

1. Henry Thiessen, cited in Tim LaHaye, *Jesus: Who Is He?* (Sisters, OR: Multnomah, 1996), p. 150.

2. Michael Green, *Man Alive!* (Downers Grove, IL: InterVarsity, 1968), pp. 23-24.

3. Barry Leventhal, "Why I Believe Jesus is the Promised Messiah," in Norman Geisler and Paul Hoffman, *Why I Am a Christian: Leading Thinkers Explain Why They Believe* (Grand Rapids, MI: Baker, 2001), p. 214.

4. Norman Geisler and Frank Turek, *I Don't Have Enough Faith to Be an Atheist* (Wheaton, IL: Crossway, 2004), pp. 290-91.

5. J.P. Moreland and Kai Nielsen, *Does God Exist? The Great Debate* (Nashville, TN: Nelson, 1990), p. 42.

6. Gary Habermas, cited in Lee Strobel, *The Case for Christ* (Grand Rapids, MI: Zondervan, 1998), p. 230.

7. Canon Westcott, "The Gospel of the Resurrection," *Illustrations*, Dallas Theological Seminary.

8. Sir Edward Clarke; cited by John Stott, *Basic Christianity* (Downers Grove, IL: InterVarsity, 1971), p. 47.

9. Cited by Wilbur Smith, *Sermons on the Christian Life*, Dallas Theological Seminary, *Illustrations*.

10. W. MacDonald and A. Farstad, *Believer's Bible Commentary* (Nashville, TN: Nelson, 1997), Logos Bible Software.

11. Anthony A. Hoekema, *The Bible and the Future* (Grand Rapids, MI: Eerdmans, 1984), p. 248.

12. J. Oswald Sanders, *Heaven: Better By Far* (Grand Rapids, MI: Discovery House, 1993), p. 91.

13. Joni Eareckson Tada, cited in Thomas Ice and Timothy J. Demy, *What the Bible Says About Heaven and Eternity* (Grand Rapids, MI: Kregel, 2000), p. 50.

14. Wayne Grudem, *Systematic Theology: An Introduction to Biblical Doctrine* (Grand Rapids, MI: Zondervan, 1994), p. 831.

15. George Sweeting, *Great Quotes and Illustrations* (Waco, TX: Word, 1985), p. 217.

Chapter 5—The Resurrection: Frequently Asked Questions

1. Thomas Ice and Timothy J. Demy, *What the Bible Says About Heaven and Eternity* (Grand Rapids, MI: Kregel, 2000), p. 25.

2. Jon Courson, *Jon Courson's Application Commentary* (Nashville, TN: Nelson, 2003), p. 1118. Albert Barnes likewise notes that use of the word "tent" for the human body indicates that the body "was of the same nature as a booth or tent, that was set up for a temporary purpose, or that was easily taken down in migrating from one place to another. It refers here to the body as the frail and temporary abode of the soul. It is not a permanent dwelling—a fixed habitation; but is liable to be taken down at any moment." See Albert Barnes, "2 Corinthians," *Notes on the New Testament* (Grand Rapids, MI: Baker, 1996), p. 104.

3. George Eldon Ladd, *The Last Things* (Grand Rapids, MI: Eerdmans, 1982), p. 37.

4. Barnes, p. 105.

5. Courson, p. 1118.

6. Paul Powell, *When the Hurt Won't Go Away* (Wheaton, IL: Victor, 1986), p. 119.

7. John Calvin, cited in John Blanchard, *Whatever Happened to Hell?* (Durham, England: Evangelical Press, 1993), p. 97.

8. See Mark Hitchcock, *55 Answers to Questions About Life after Death* (Sisters, OR: Multnomah, 2005), p. 216.

9. Norman Geisler, "Church/Last Things," *Systematic Theology*, vol. 4 (Minneapolis, MN: Bethany House, 2005), p. 309.

10. Geisler, p. 311; see also *Tim LaHaye Prophecy Study Bible* (Chattanooga, TN: AMG, 2001), p. 1536.

11. John MacArthur, *The Glory of Heaven* (Wheaton, IL: Crossway, 1996), p. 115.

12. Hitchcock, pp. 195-96.

13. Randy Alcorn, *Heaven* (Wheaton, IL: Tyndale, 2004), p. 295.

14. Alcorn, p. 283.

15. John MacArthur, *The MacArthur New Testament Commentary: Revelation 12-22* (Chicago, IL: Moody, 2000), p. 267.

16. *The New International Dictionary of New Testament Theology,* ed. Colin Brown, vol. 2 (Grand Rapids, MI: Zondervan, 1979), p. 45.

17. John MacArthur suggests that even so, "the saints in heavenly glory will not be able to comprehend *all* the infinite majesty of God's wondrous being. But they will see all that glorified beings are able to comprehend. Is it any wonder that Paul, thinking of the glory of heaven, had 'the desire to depart and be with Christ, for that is very much better' (Philippians 1:23)?" See MacArthur, *Revelation 12-22,* p. 267.

Chapter 6—Heaven: Frequently Asked Questions

1. Merrill F. Unger, *Beyond the Crystal Ball* (Chicago, IL: Moody, 1973), p. 173.

2. Unger, p. 173.

3. John Gill, "Hebrews 11:13-15" in *The Online Bible* (electronic media).

4. Wayne Grudem, *Systematic Theology: An Introduction to Biblical Doctrine* (Grand Rapids, MI: Zondervan, 1994), pp. 1159-60.

5. Kenneth Boa and Robert Bowman, *Sense and Nonsense About Heaven and Hell* (Grand Rapids, MI: Zondervan, 2007), p. 166.

6. Anthony Hoekema, cited in Randy Alcorn, *Heaven* (Wheaton, IL: Tyndale, 2004), p. 111.

7. Norman Geisler, "Church/Last Things," *Systematic Theology,* vol. 4 (Minneapolis: Bethany House, 2005), p. 313.

8. Geisler, *Systematic Theology,* p. 313.

9. See Geisler, *Systematic Theology,* p. 298.

10. Norman Geisler, Wayne House, and Max Herrera, *The Battle for God* (Grand Rapids, MI: Kregel, 2001), p. 24.

11. Geisler, House, and Herrera, p. 92.

12. Geisler, *Systematic Theology,* p. 316, insert added, emphasis added.

13. Elaine Allegrini, "Heaven Gained a Glorious Angel?" *The Enterprise,* December 13, 2007.

14. J. Sidlow Baxter, *The Other Side of Death* (Grand Rapids, MI: Kregel, 1987), p. 53.

15. John MacArthur, *The Glory of Heaven* (Wheaton, IL: Crossway, 1996), p. 56.

16. A.C. Gaebelein, *What the Bible Says About Angels* (Grand Rapids, MI: Baker, 1987), p. 81.

17. Isbon T. Beckwith, *The Apocalypse of John* (Grand Rapids, MI: Baker, 1967), pp. 312-13.

18. Lewis Sperry Chafer, *Systematic Theology,* ed. John F. Walvoord (Wheaton, IL: Victor, 1989), p. 284.

19. R.C. Sproul, *Now, That's a Good Question* (Wheaton, IL: Tyndale, 1996), p. 291.

20. Peter Kreeft, *Everything You Ever Wanted to Know About Heaven* (San Francisco, CA: Ignatius Press, 1990), p. 45.

21. Peter Kreeft, cited in Mark Hitchcock, *55 Answers to Questions About Life After Death* (Colorado Springs, CO: Multnomah, 2005), p. 230.

22. Hitchcock, p. 229.

23. C.S. Lewis, cited in Kreeft, p. 45.

24. Alcorn, pp. 375-85.

25. Geisler, *Systematic Theology,* p. 312.

26. Geisler, *Systematic Theology,* p. 312.

27. MacArthur, p. 83.

28. See J. Oswald Sanders, *Heaven: Better By Far* (Grand Rapids, MI: Discovery House, 1993), p. 67.

29. These items are derived from Carey Kinsolving, "What Does Heaven Look Like?" parts 1, 2, and 3, *Creator's Syndicate,* January 14, 21, and 28, 2008.

Chapter 7—The Splendor of the Eternal City: The New Jerusalem

1. Cited in Douglas Connelly, *What the Bible Really Says: After Life* (Downers Grove, IL: InterVarsity, 1995), p. 92, insert added.

2. "When We All Get to Heaven," words by Eliza E. Hewitt, music by Emily D. Watson (1898).

3. Henry M. Morris, *The Biblical Basis for Modern Science* (Grand Rapids, MI: Baker, 1984), p. 156.

4. Morris, p. 156.

5. John MacArthur, *The Superiority of Christ* (Chicago, IL: Moody, 1986), pp. 33-34.

6. Anne Graham Lotz, *Heaven: My Father's House* (Nashville, TN: Nelson, 2001), p. 49.

7. Randy Alcorn, *Heaven* (Wheaton, IL: Tyndale, 2004), p. 241.

8. J. Boudreau, *The Happiness of Heaven* (Rockford, IL: Tan Books and Publishers, 1984), p. vii.

9. John F. Walvoord and Roy Zuck, *The Bible Knowledge Commentary* (Wheaton, IL: Victor, 1985), Logos Bible Software.

10. Millard Erickson, *Christian Theology* (Grand Rapids, MI: Baker, 1987), p. 1229.

11. George Marsden, *Jonathan Edwards: A Life* (New Haven, CT: Yale University, 2003), p. 98.

12. John F. Walvoord, *The Revelation of Jesus Christ* (Chicago, IL: Moody, 1966), p. 325.

13. Walvoord, *The Revelation of Jesus Christ*, p. 325.

14. A.T. Pierson, cited in Walvoord, *The Revelation of Jesus Christ*, p. 332.

15. Peter Kreeft, *Everything You Ever Wanted to Know About Heaven* (San Francisco, CA: Ignatius Press, 1990), p. 47.

16. Kenneth Boa and Robert Bowman write, "It is entirely possible to affirm the material reality of the New Earth as a realm for resurrected human beings while denying that the description of the New Jerusalem is meant to be taken literally." See their book, *Sense and Nonsense About Heaven and Hell* (Grand Rapids, MI: Zondervan, 2007), p. 165.

17. Lotz, p. 48.

18. John MacArthur, *The Glory of Heaven* (Wheaton, IL: Crossway, 1996), pp. 107-08.

19. Alcorn, p. 242.

20. Connelly, p. 98.

21. Alcorn, p. 242.

22. Lotz, p. 48.

23. Mark Hitchcock, *55 Answers to Questions About Life After Death* (Colorado Springs, CO: Multnomah, 2005), p. 34.

24. See MacArthur, *The Glory of Heaven,* p. 107.

25. *Tim LaHaye Prophecy Study Bible* (Chattanooga, TN: AMG, 2001), p. 1535.

26. John F. Walvoord, *The Church in Prophecy* (Grand Rapids, MI: Zondervan, 1964), p. 164.

27. Albert Barnes, "Revelation," *Notes on the New Testament* (Grand Rapids, MI: Baker, 1996), p. 453.

28. Walvoord, *The Revelation of Jesus Christ*, p. 330.

29. Cited in Tim LaHaye, *Revelation: Illustrated and Made Plain* (Grand Rapids, MI: Zondervan, 1975), p. 315.

30. Bruce Shelley, *Theology for Ordinary People* (Downers Grove, IL: InterVarsity, 1994), p. 212.

31. Wilbur Smith, cited in "Revelation," *Wycliffe Bible Commentary* (Chicago, IL: Moody, 1960), p. 1524.

Chapter 8—The New Heavens and the New Earth

1. *Tim LaHaye Prophecy Study Bible* (Chattanooga, TN: AMG, 2001), p. 1534.

2. Albert Barnes, "Revelation," *Notes on the New Testament* (Grand Rapids, MI: Baker, 1996), p. 454.

3. John F. Walvoord, *The Prophecy Knowledge Handbook* (Wheaton, IL: Victor, 1990), Logos Bible Software.

4. John MacArthur, *The Glory of Heaven* (Wheaton, IL: Crossway, 1996), p. 90.

5. John F. Walvoord notes: "The verb *make*...means 'to make, form, or construct' and is a common verb occurring many times in the New Testament for a work of accomplishment." Truly, the new heavens and new earth will be a phenomenal work of accomplishment. See his book, *The Revelation of Jesus Christ* (Chicago: Moody, 1966), p. 315.

6. Kenneth Boa and Robert Bowman, *Sense and Nonsense About Heaven and Hell* (Grand Rapids, MI: Zondervan, 2007), pp. 166-67.

7. See Boa and Bowman, pp. 166-67.

8. Boa and Bowman, pp. 166-67.

9. Anthony A. Hoekema, *The Bible and the Future* (Grand Rapids, MI: Eerdmans, 1984), p. 280.

10. William Hendrickson, cited in J. Oswald Sanders, *Heaven: Better By Far* (Grand Rapids, MI: Discovery House, 1993), p. 131.

11. Sanders, p. 134.

12. John Piper, cited in Randy Alcorn, *Heaven* (Wheaton, IL: Tyndale, 2004), p. 125.

13. Merrill F. Unger, *Beyond the Crystal Ball* (Chicago, IL: Moody, 1973), p. 167.

14. Alcorn, p. 79.

15. Alcorn, p. 88, emphasis added.

16. Alcorn, p. 89.

17. Barnes, p. 443.

18. John MacArthur, *Because the Time Is Near* (Chicago, IL: Moody, 2007), p. 315.

19. Hoekema, p. 285.

20. Mark Hitchcock, *55 Answers to Questions About Life After Death* (Sisters, OR: Multnomah, 2005) p. 189.

21. Morrow, pp. 329-30.

22. See J. Boudreau, *The Happiness of Heaven* (Rockford, IL: Tan Books and Publishers, 1984), p. 135.

23. MacArthur, *The Glory of Heaven*, p. 137.

24. *Tim LaHaye Prophecy Study Bible*, p. 1535.

25. Barnes, p. 445.

Chapter 9—The Blessing of Heaven for Believers

1. J.C. Ryle, cited in John MacArthur, *The Glory of Heaven* (Wheaton, IL: Crossway, 1996), p. 259.

2. Albert Barnes, "Revelation," *Notes on the New Testament* (Grand Rapids, MI: Baker, 1996), p. 444.

3. John F. Walvoord, *The Revelation of Jesus Christ* (Chicago, IL: Moody, 1966), p. 315.

4. Barnes, pp. 444-45.

5. John F. Walvoord, *The Prophecy Knowledge Handbook* (Wheaton, IL: Victor, 1990), Logos Bible Software.

6. John MacArthur, *Because the Time Is Near* (Chicago, IL: Moody, 2007), p. 318.

7. A.T. Robertson says that God's wiping of every tear shows the tender side of God, much like a nurturing mother. See A.T. Robertson, *Word Pictures in the New Testament* (Nashville, tn: Holman, 2000), p. 689.

8. *Tim LaHaye Prophecy Study Bible* (Chattanooga, TN: AMG, 2001), p. 1535.

9. Randal Rauser, "How Could I Be Happy in Heaven with a Loved One in Hell?" *Faith Today,* January/February 2008.

10. MacArthur, *The Glory of Heaven*, p. 97.

11. Mark Hitchcock, *55 Answers to Questions About Life After Death* (Sisters, OR: Multnomah, 2005), p. 185.

12. See Donald Barnhouse, *Revelation: An Expository Commentary* (Grand Rapids, MI: Zondervan, 1971), p. 401.

13. Note that there are some Christians who have held that even when we get to heaven, we will not be able to behold God. They cite Exodus 33:20, where God said, "You cannot see my face, for no one may see me and live." We read of Jesus, "No one has ever seen God, but God the One and Only, who is at the Father's side, has made him known" (John 1:18). First Timothy 6:15-16 makes reference "the King of kings and Lord of lords, who alone is immortal and who lives in unapproachable light, whom no one has seen or can see." In this book, these verses are interpreted in a way compatible with the view that we shall dwell face-to-face with God, something made possible by our glorious resurrection bodies.

14. Bruce Milne, *Know the Truth* (Downers Grove, IL: InterVarsity, 1982), p. 278.

15. "Face to Face with Christ, My Savior," lyrics by Carrie Breck, music by Grant Tullar (1898). Only the first and last stanzas along with the chorus are quoted.

16. Randy Alcorn, *Heaven* (Wheaton, IL: Tyndale, 2004), pp. 169-70.

17. Barry Morrow, *Heaven Observed: Glimpses of Transcendence in Everyday Life* (Colorado Springs, CO: NavPress, 2001), p. 324.

18. J.C. Ryle, *Heaven* (Ross-shire, Great Britain: Christian Focus Publications, 2000), p. 40.

19. See Anne Graham Lotz, *Heaven: My Father's House* (Nashville, TN: Nelson, 2001), p. 94.

20. Richard Baxter, *Saints' Everlasting Rest* (Philadelphia, PA: Lippincott, 1859), pp. 54,19.

21. J. Sidlow Baxter, *The Other Side of Death* (Grand Rapids, MI: Kregel, 1987), p. 54.

22. Joni Eareckson Tada, *Heaven: Your Real Home* (Grand Rapids, MI: Zondervan, 1995), p. 64.

23. Douglas Connelly, *What the Bible Really Says: After Life* (Downers Grove, IL: InterVarsity, 1995), p. 101.

24. Thomas Ice and Timothy J. Demy, *What the Bible Says About Heaven and Eternity* (Grand Rapids, MI: Kregel, 2000), p. 24.

25. Peter Kreeft, *Everything You Ever Wanted to Know About Heaven* (San Francisco, CA: Ignatius, 1990), p. 27.

26. Sam Storms, cited in Alcorn, pp. 172-73.

27. Hitchcock, p. 175.

28. Jonathan Edwards, cited in Alcorn, p. 302.

29. Ryle, pp. 24-25.

30. Ryle, pp. 24-25.

Chapter 10—Heaven for Those Who Can't Believe

1. G.N.M. Collins, "Infant Salvation," in *Evangelical Dictionary of Theology*, ed. Walter A. Elwell (Grand Rapids, MI: Baker, 1984), p. 560.

2. Robert Lightner, *Heaven for Those Who Can't Believe* (Schaumburg, IL: Regular Baptist Press, 1977), p. 10; see also Charles C. Ryrie, *Basic Theology* (Wheaton, IL: Victor, 1986), pp. 218-21; Louis Berkhof, *Manual of Christian Doctrine* (Grand Rapids, MI: Eerdmans, 1983), pp. 143-45; Henry Clarence Thiessen, *Lectures in Systematic Theology* (Grand Rapids, MI: Eerdmans, 1981), pp. 173-82.

3. Lightner, p. 10.

4. Millard J. Erickson, *Christian Theology* (Grand Rapids, MI: Baker, 1985), p. 639.

5. Lightner, p. 18.

6. Lightner, pp. 19-25; see also Ron Rhodes, *Christ Before the Manger: The Life and Times of the Preincarnate Christ* (Grand Rapids, MI: Baker, 1992), pp. 43-48.

7. As noted previously, however, God does not exercise His love at the expense of His holiness. The infant's sin problem must be dealt with. The solution is that at the moment the infant dies—and not before—the benefits of Jesus' atoning death on the cross are applied to him or her. And at that moment, the infant becomes saved and is immediately issued into the presence of God in heaven. This view is in keeping both with the love of God and His holiness.

8. Lightner, p. 22.

9. J.I. Packer, *Knowing God* (Downers Grove, IL: InterVarsity, 1973), p. 138; see also Lightner, p. 23.

10. That David was going to heaven is clear from other passages. For example, David affirmed, "I will dwell in the house of the Lord forever" (Psalm 23:6).

11. See John Blanchard, *Whatever Happened to Hell?* (Durham, England: Evangelical Press, 1993), pp. 113-14.

12. Lightner, p. 33.

13. J. Sidlow Baxter, *The Other Side of Death* (Grand Rapids, MI: Kregel, 1987), p. 73.

14. Kenneth Boa and Robert Bowman, *Sense and Nonsense About Heaven and Hell* (Grand Rapids, MI: Zondervan, 2007), pp. 135-36.

15. J. Oswald Sanders, *Heaven: Better By Far* (Grand Rapids, MI: Discovery House, 1993), p. 52.

Chapter 11—Rewards for Faithful Service

1. Barry Morrow, *Heaven Observed: Glimpses of Transcendence in Everyday Life* (Colorado Springs, CO: NavPress, 2001), p. 334.

2. John Wesley, *The Nature of Salvation* (Minneapolis: Bethany House, 1987), p. 134.

3. In recent years the idea that God is a judge has fallen out of favor. Most people prefer to focus almost exclusively on the love of God. Certainly it is true that God is a God of love. But He is also a holy and righteous judge. This has always been true of Him. In the New Testament, for example, we find that judgment falls on the chief priests and Pharisees for rejecting Jesus Christ (Matthew 21:43), on Ananias and Sapphira for lying to God (Acts 5), on Herod for his self-exalting pride (Acts 12:21-23), and on Christians in Corinth who were afflicted with illness in response to their irreverence in connection with the Lord's Supper (1 Corinthians 11:29-32). God truly *is* a God of judgment. For us to forget or ignore this fact is to do so at our own peril. God *will* hold all of us accountable for the things done in this life.

4. J. Oswald Sanders, *Heaven: Better By Far* (Grand Rapids, MI: Discovery House, 1993), p. 82.

5. See George Marsden, *Jonathan Edwards: A Life* (New Haven, CT: Yale University, 2003), p. 191.

6. Douglas Connelly, *What the Bible Really Says: After Life* (Downers Grove, IL: InterVarsity, 1995), p. 119.

7. Morrow, p. 336.

8. John Walvoord, *The Church in Prophecy* (Grand Rapids, MI: Zondervan, 1974), p. 145.

9. Cited in Charles C. Ryrie, *Basic Theology* (Wheaton, IL: Victor, 1986), p. 513.

10. Walvoord, p. 148.

11. Walvoord, p. 149.

12. Connelly, p. 118.

13. Merrill F. Unger, *Beyond the Crystal Ball* (Chicago, IL: Moody, 1973), p. 63.

14. Walvoord, p. 150.

15. Walvoord, p. 150.

16. Wesley, p. 135.

17. John Blanchard, *Whatever Happened to Hell?* (Durham, England: Evangelical Press, 1993), p. 116.

18. See Mark Hitchcock, *55 Answers to Questions About Life After Death* (Sisters, OR: Multnomah Books, 2005), pp. 148-49.

19. Arnold Fruchtenbaum, *The Footsteps of the Messiah* (San Antonio, TX: Ariel Press, 1982), p. 158.

20. Fruchtenbaum, p. 160.

21. Fruchtenbaum, p. 158.

22. Fruchtenbaum, p. 159.

23. Fruchtenbaum, p. 159.

24. Hitchcock, p. 151.

25. Norman Geisler, "Church/Last Things," *Systematic Theology*, vol. 4 (Minneapolis: Bethany House, 2005), p. 310.

26. J. Dwight. Pentecost, *Things to Come* (Grand Rapids, MI: Zondervan, 1974), p. 226.

Chapter 12—Helping Those Who Grieve

1. "Grief," *Illustrations*, Dallas Theological Seminary.

2. John F. Walvoord and Roy Zuck, *The Bible Knowledge Commentary* (Wheaton, IL: Victor, 1985). Logos Bible Software.

3. Cited in Bill Donahue and Russ Robinson, *Building a Church of Small Groups* (Grand Rapids, MI: Zondervan, 2001), p. 61.

4. Rick Taylor, *When Life Is Changed Forever* (Eugene, OR: Harvest House, 1992), p. 120.

5. Taylor, p. 120.

6. C.S. Lewis, *A Grief Observed*; cited in Taylor, p. 50.

7. Sharan Morris, *Grief and How to Live with It*, p. 18; cited in Haddon W. Robinson, *Grief* (Grand Rapids, MI: Zondervan, 1976), p. 9.

8. *Home Living*, May 1980. Cited in *Illustrations*, Dallas Theological Seminary.

Chapter 13—Looking Toward Eternity

1. Saint Teresa, cited in Lee Strobel, *The Case for Faith* (Grand Rapids, MI: Zondervan, 2000), p. 47.

2. John Wenham, *The Enigma of Evil: Can We Believe in the Goodness of God?* (Grand Rapids, MI: Zondervan, 1985), p. 55.

3. Philip Yancey, *Where Is God When It Hurts?* (Grand Rapids, MI: Zondervan, 1977), p. 176.

4. J.I. Packer, ed. *Alive to God: Studies in Spirituality* (Downers Grove, IL: InterVarsity, 1992), p. 162.

5. Packer, p. 171.

6. Packer, p. 171.

7. Packer, p. 163.

8. Packer, p. 164.

9. Packer, p. 165.

10. Packer, p. 165.

11. Richard Baxter; cited in Packer, p. 167.

12. Richard Baxter, *Saints' Everlasting Rest* (Philadelphia, PA: Lippincott, 1859), pp. 25-26.

13. J.C. Ryle, *Heaven* (Ross-shire, Great Britain: Christian Focus Publications, 2000), p. 47.

14. Ryle, pp. 83-84.

15. Gary R. Habermas and J.P. Moreland, *Immortality: The Other Side of Death* (Nashville, TN: Nelson, 1992), p. 185.

16. Mark Buchanan, *Things Unseen: Living in Light of Forever* (Sisters, OR: Multnomah, 2002), pp. 22-23.

17. Buchanan, p. 23.

18. J. Oswald Sanders, *Heaven: Better by Far* (Grand Rapids, MI: Discovery House, 1993), p. 15.

19. Randy Alcorn, *Heaven* (Wheaton, IL: Tyndale, 2004), p. 444.

20. Henri Nouwen, *Our Greatest Gift: A Meditation on Dying and Caring* (San Francisco, CA: HarperSanFrancisco, 1994), pp. 19-20.

21. John MacArthur, *The Glory of Heaven* (Wheaton, IL: Crossway, 1996), p. 48.

22. Habermas and Moreland, p. 186.

23. Greek scholar Ralph Earle tells us that the phrase "set your affection" literally carries the idea, "to have in mind, be mindful of, think of." It carries the idea, "be intent on," or "to direct one's mind on." See Ralph Earle, *Word Meanings in the New Testament* (Peabody, MA: Hendrickson, 1986), p. 357.

24. Alcorn, p. 20.

25. See Alcorn, p. 20.

26. Alcorn, p. 21.

27. Alister McGrath, *A Brief History of Heaven* (Malden, MA: Blackwell, 2003), pp. 12-13.

28. Arnold Fruchtenbaum, *The Footsteps of the Messiah* (San Antonio, TX: Ariel Press, 1982), p. 706.

29. John Calvin, *Institutes of the Christian Religion,* ed. John T. McNeill (Philadelphia: Westminster Press, n.d.), p. 590.

30. John Wesley, *The Nature of Spiritual Growth* (Minneapolis, Bethany House, 1987), p. 189.

31. Charles Spurgeon; cited by Jim Elliot, *Shadow of the Almighty* (Grand Rapids, MI: Zondervan, 1970), p. 83.

32. Wayne Grudem, *Systematic Theology: An Introduction to Biblical Doctrine* (Grand Rapids, MI: Zondervan, 1994), p. 813.

33. Sanders, p. 31.

34. Sanders, p. 21.

35. J. Sidlow Baxter, *The Other Side of Death* (Grand Rapids, MI: Kregel, 1987), pp. 66-67.

36. "Fear of Death," *Illustrations,* Dallas Theological Seminary.

Postscript: An Invitation to Believe

1. Associated Press, "How Do You Spend $1.5 Billion a Year?" Reported at cbsnews.com, June 27, 2006.

2. J.C. Ryle, *Heaven* (Ross-shire, Great Britain: Christian Focus Publications, 2000), pp. 66-67.

Appendix B: The "Great Cloud of Witnesses": Are We Being Watched from Heaven?

1. *The Wycliffe Bible Commentary,* eds. C.F. Pfeiffer and E.F. Harrison (Chicago, IL: Moody, 1962), in Logos Bible Software.

2. Randy Alcorn, *Heaven* (Wheaton, IL: Tyndale, 2004), p. 70.

3. See Hitchcock, *55 Answers to Questions About Life After Death* (Sisters, OR: Multnomah Books, 2005), p. 182.

4. Peter Kreeft, *Everything You Ever Wanted to Know About Heaven* (San Francisco, CA: Ignatius, 1990), p. 32.

5. W. MacDonald and A. Farstad, *Believer's Bible Commentary* (Nashville, TN: Nelson, 1997), in Logos Bible Software, insert added.

Appendix C: Assessing Alleged Firsthand Reports About Heaven

1. See Mark Hitchcock, *55 Answers to Questions About Life After Death* (Sisters, OR: Multnomah, 2005), p. 138.

2. See Hitchcock, p. 139.

3. John Ankerberg and John Weldon, *The Facts on Life After Death* (Eugene, OR: Harvest House, 1992), pp. 10,11.

4. Kenneth Ring, cited in Ankerberg and Weldon, p. 21.

5. Rodney Clapp, "Rumors of Heaven," *Christianity Today,* 7 October 1988, p. 20.

6. Jerry Yamamoto, "The Near-Death Experience," *Christian Research Journal,* Spring 1992, p. 5.

7. Yamamoto, p. 5.

8. Gary R. Habermas and J.P. Moreland, *Immortality: The Other Side of Death* (Nashville, TN: Nelson, 1992), p. 93.

Other Great Harvest House Reading

by Ron Rhodes